YOUR MIND AT SIEGE

Exploring the Conundrum of Consciousness, Artificial Intelligence through the Lens of the Diamond Sutra

DAVID JAMES
(The UnMonk)

Contents

Preface

I'd like to make it clear from the start that this book is not an academic dissertation, and should not be approached as such. It serves as a written adaptation of my podcast series, *"Commentary on the Diamond Sutra in a World of Artificial Intelligence"*, which was broadcasted from 2020 to 2022. In response to numerous requests from global listeners for a text version, the chapters have been enhanced with context and references, allowing readers to delve into the expanded content at a more leisurely pace.

The Diamond Sutra, as I've repeatedly stressed in my podcasts, has a fragmented structure and a recursive narrative. This led to recurrent themes as I navigated its disjointed verses. The podcast's listener demographics varied as the podcast progressed, with repeated questions suggesting a common global interest. Thus, I've retained these repetitions, derived from the audience's queries, to maintain the spoken material's integrity. This intentional redundancy should enable readers to grasp the main theme of my critique of the Diamond Sutra, regardless of their starting chapter.

The podcasts were born during the pandemic, a time when physical interaction was challenging, leading to a surge in users across the world on platforms like ClubHouse/ClubDeck and Discord.

Such platforms, however, allowed anyone with a microphone to anonymously speak on any subject, showcasing their expertise or lack thereof. This trend persists today among many Neo-Vedantins and Neo-Buddhists. In reaction to the prevalent alternative facts being presented by exegetes in many rooms that cropped up, that included YouTube, a devoted collective of critical thinkers soon congregated in *"The Art of Dying"* room which I moderated. Here, we collaboratively engaged in my discussions on Consciousness, dissecting the most recent discoveries from the past 150 years. These discussions started with a primary audience of Neo-Buddhists and Neo-Advaitins who were drawn to discussions on early Buddhist texts like the Diamond Sutra. As entrenched beliefs surfaced, I urged listeners to challenge these views with evidence and probing questions. This shift promoted a more erudite and sceptical audience, intrigued by contemporary developments in clinical psychology and neurosciences, rendering age-old religious dogma obsolete. Soon my commentary began to explore Artificial Intelligence (AI) as a point of contrast with human understanding of the Self and our cosmic place, speculating whether our creation – AI -could replace us.

My talks included an approach to examining humanity's subjugation of Consciousness, studying how we, as humans, often surrender our consciousness to external authority that appears intelligent. This approach to viewing intelligence and consciousness prompts us to reconsider our relationship with external authority.

Furthermore, I delved into a fundamental quandary that we humans wrestle with. This quandary revolves around the discord between the nature of causality - the principle that everything has a cause and an effect, and is effectively out of our control and comprehension - and the version of causality that our cognitive apparatus can be the engine of its own causality. The difference between these two can often create a dissonance that is both intriguing and challenging.

Throughout the discussions, I explore cutting-edge developments in evolutionary biology and neuroscience. These sections aren't just cursory overviews. They're aimed at opening up the latest thoughts and insights in these fields. By probing these ideas, I hope to shed light on the questions about consciousness and causality that were raised, providing a more nuanced understanding of these complex issues.

These scientific studies discussed may not appeal to the religious, just as the Diamond Sutra's philosophical implications may not captivate the scientifically inclined. But cross-pollination of concepts from both sides was sparked during the podcasts and ensuing ClubHouse/ClubDeck discussions that followed, and these are reflected in the broad scope of these chapters.

Addressing both parties in spoken format was a challenge. In this written form even more formidable as I struggled to retain the spoken word's integrity and consistency and present a style palatable to all.

This book doesn't cater to those with a cultural or religious bias, nor does it advocate for specific philosophical standpoints. Rather, it questions our collective psychosis and blind adherence to all canonical texts and AI's purported superiority to our own cognition, which have relegated humanity to a state of subservience to the encroaching TechnoUtopia.

For those content with the way things are and reluctant to change, this book could indeed pose a formidable challenge.

I have sought no endorsement from religious or philosophical figures—the content herein is purely my creation and the product of my own cognition. Any inaccuracies are solely mine, dismissible as opinionated at worst, or original at best.

Since the inaugural printing of the Diamond Sutra on May 11th, 868 AD, in Chinese, there have been countless editions and translations, each spawning its unique interpretation. For simplicity's sake, I have opted to use the English version translated by A.F. Price and Wong Mou-Lam.

If we have previously met online during our discussions, your questions were instrumental in refining my answers and bringing this book out, and for that, I offer you my gratitude.

I am easily reachable via the Matrix for further engagement.

Finally, I humbly thank you for purchasing my book and investing your time.

DJ/The UnMonk

Bangalore, India

Acknowledgments

My profound gratitude extends to my cherished wife and son, the silent warriors who have faithfully accompanied me on every ascent and descent of this project. Their unwavering encouragement and steadfast belief in my work have been my lighthouse in the storm, their patience an enduring testament to their faith in me. Notably, their exceptional care and support during my daunting tenure in the ICU were invaluable. Without their resilience and fortitude, the journey would have been significantly more challenging.

Next, I offer my sincere appreciation to the energetic community at ClubHouse/ClubDeck. Their persistent curiosity and thoughtful questions have been the lifeblood of the podcast, instilling it with richness and complexity. Their encouragement and enthusiasm were the sparks that fuelled the transformation of the spoken word into the pages of this book. Their active engagement has truly elevated this project, transcending the confines of traditional audio content.

I am deeply indebted to Deepak and Deepika Doraiswamy of Bimba, The Art Ashram, whose sharp perspectives, and rigorous scrutiny have immensely enriched the quality of the final manuscript. They cleverly identified overlooked elements and significantly contributed to refining the narrative, adding depth, clarity, and precision to the work.

I also wish to acknowledge the astute listeners whose keen attention to detail has led to valuable corrections and insights. While it is impossible to acknowledge every one of you individually, rest assured, your contributions have been instrumental to this project. You have nudged me toward continual refinement and improvement of the content, for which I am profoundly grateful.

Furthermore, my deep gratitude extends to the small band of devoted followers of Osho and 'J.K.'. Our thoughtful exchanges on the theme of "fingers pointing to the moon" have been a beacon of understanding and insight. Your probing questions have inspired me to seamlessly interweave those profound discussions into the fabric of this book.

By extension, I would be remiss not to express my gratitude for the spiritual lineages of Osho, 'J.K', and other spiritual pioneers who dared to venture beyond traditional spiritual dogma. Echoes of their profound teachings permeate this book, subtly infusing their wisdom into its fundamental narrative.

To all of you, my heartfelt thanks. Your invaluable contributions have imbued this book with a tapestry of spiritual wisdom and depth. I ardently hope that the readers will glean as much enlightenment and joy from these insights as I have done during our enlightening dialogues.

Finally, to everyone acknowledged and those unmentioned, I offer my profound gratitude. This book is as much a product of your efforts as it is mine. It truly takes an entire planet to birth a book, and I am honoured to have been part of such a dynamic and magnanimous community. A sincere and heartfelt thank you to you all.

Introduction

The Diamond Sutra, renowned as one of the earliest Mahayana Buddhist texts, hails from antiquity. Typically translated from its original Sanskrit title as "Diamond Cutter," a notable number of interpreters prefer "The Cutter of Diamonds." This latter translation resonates with the idea of a Mind capable of slicing through the rigidity of certainty and conditioned beliefs, thereby unveiling the true essence of Reality.

It is generally accepted that the text emerged from a sermon by Siddhartha Gautama delivered to a congregation of monks in Northern India, despite a scholarly consensus that these exact words did not flow from the Buddha himself. Instead, the text is seen as a creative manifestation of the Buddha's teachings, designed with the purpose of proselytization of spiritual concepts and ideas to a wider audience.

The Diamond Sutra embodies a style of writing prevalent in the spiritual literature of its time, largely due to the widespread adoption of printing. As such, the Sutra encapsulates its era and environment, mirroring the cultural and spiritual climate of ancient India.

A common issue with ancient texts lies in the constraints of language—it falls short in conveying the inexpressible, leading to misinterpretation of transcendence as a material entity or an object. Within our private mental theatre, language fails to grasp these subjective experiences, and any attempt to translate these experiences will always fall short, thus creating confusion and diminishing meaning.

The Diamond Sutra masterfully employs irony to express meanings contrary to their literal interpretation; when read this way, the Sutra avoids the pitfall of nihilism. Disagreement over the use of irony has resulted in inadequate translations that objectify personal experiences, promoting the misguided belief that nominal descriptions and labels adequately express our inner realm.

The Diamond Sutra's use of "No-Thing" to signify emptiness proposes the continuous change and interdependence of all things, asserting our concepts and labels as mere mental constructs. While this can seem nihilistic, it ignores the existence of inherent meaning or purpose in our interactions with phenomena that give us our subjective experiences. The identification of the Self as an object is a long-standing error that has percolated throughout the centuries. *(One chapter is dedicated to exploring how language distorts our understanding of consciousness).*

Many who espouse the absolutist viewpoint of "no-self" or "nihilism" results in rigidity and disengagement from real-time interaction with Universal Consciousness. Similarly, dismissing any critique of ancient canons is another sign of absolutism that can lead to the stagnation of culture.

The enduring existential question—what is our purpose here?—is widely shared, with many dedicating their lives to pondering over Cause and Effect. Our cognition greatly influences our thought processes that give us insight, acting as our only foothold in the doorway of consciousness. However, by neglecting our own cognitive capabilities and insights, we risk falling into a mindset that life merely happens to us, rather than recognizing our active role in creating our future.

In today's era of pervasive Artificial Intelligence (AI), we are prompted to question our own humanness and identity. With AI already surpassing human performance in many tasks, we are forced to contemplate the implications of a total AI takeover. Are we prepared for machines to outsmart us? As physicist **Stephen Hawking** warned, AI could potentially be humanity's worst calamity, even worse than the threat of climate change or a nuclear holocaust.

This shift towards AI places humanity at a critical juncture of our ongoing inquiry. AI challenges our individual and collective relevance, prompting us to ask if we are prepared for a world dominated by our own creations. Can we coexist with AI without compromising our sense of existence and autonomy?

Many spiritual preachers describe their metaphysics as being derived from an eternal or perennial religion, asserting its constancy. However, in a world marked by rapid change, how do we reconcile this Universe's constancy with the reality of constant change? It is imperative that in this ever-changing flux, we work towards understanding change because, much like any other biological entity or system, the Universe strives for expansion and evolution.

With the even faster change that AI brings, we need to truly comprehend what AI is, and equally importantly, what it isn't, and cultivate a harmonious coexistence.

In conclusion, we must move beyond reliance on texts and teachings, instead seeking direct, experiential knowledge. We must transcend our evolutionary path derived from our instinct and fear-based conformity to emerge as creative and innovative pioneers.

We must tap into the wisdom of lived experience and understanding 'Embodied Consciousness', which gives us true meaning than merely speculating on disembodied consciousness and esoteric concepts.

Much of these ideas will be expanded upon in subsequent chapters, and I warmly invite you to join me as we traverse through the Diamond Sutra examining our existence in the era of A.I. We will first explore this text as it emerged from its real historical background that could provide better context, but also as a tool to scrutinize our own relevance and devise strategies to navigate the tidal wave of impending change.

Chapter 1

Real History and Context

Contrary to popular belief, the Buddha's emergence in North India did not come out of a vacuum, nor did his teachings spread by magic. Grasping the popularity of his doctrine demands insight into the era's context and his lineage. Curiously, many Buddhists overlook the backdrop of the Diamond Sutra and the genesis of the early Pali Canon[1]. The **Shurangama Sutra**[2], an underrated text, highlights the crucial role our surroundings and experiences play in shaping our spiritual and religious beliefs:

> *"It is said, Dharma does not arise alone. Relying on conditions it is born. The Way is not practiced in vain. Meeting conditions, there is a response"*

which asserts that our religious and spiritual experiences *and our perceptions of reality* arise from our interpretations of our encounters with the environment..

Dispelling myths and understanding the Sutras and their origins demands delving into the Buddha's life and his era. For instance, assassination attempts on the Buddha hint at his presence being perceived as a threat likely due to massive crowds drawn by his sermons. Why target a renunciate if he were not deemed a political menace?

---

1.   The Pali Canon, or the Tripitaka, is the earliest collection of Buddhist scriptures and forms the doctrinal foundation of Theravada Buddhism.

2.   The Shurangama Sutra, an influential Mahayana text, explores the nature of reality, the mind, and the path to enlightenment.

South Asia's kingdoms, circa 500-350 BCE, brimmed with political strife and warring tribal chiefs. During this epoch, earlier Buddhas emerged, rooted in Scythian, Greek, and philosophies[3]. Etymological analyses of Pali and Sanskrit texts reveal a syncretic fusion and overlapping ideas from various cultures. The much-loved 8-fold path and 4 noble truths share parallels with the Zoroastrian tripartite path —*Humata, Hukhata, Havarashta*[4]—predating the Buddha by centuries. The Pali Canon, a compendium of Buddhist theology, originated from this melding world, and, by most estimates, was codified half a millennium post-Buddha.

Greco - Afghan Statue of the Buddha

---

3. Greco-Buddhism - Wikipedia

4. Humata, Hukhta, Hvarshta are three Avestan words which encapsulate the ethical goals of Zoroastrianism. They are commonly translated as Good Thoughts, Good Words, and Good Deeds. They are found in the Avesta, the sacred book of the Zoroastrians.

Gandhara Buddha

Furthermore, contemporary research posits that the Buddha was an Iranian-Afghan political refugee who may have unnerved kings who saw his crowd-pulling power as perilous. Red hair and blue eyes attributed to him fuel genealogical inquiries, suggesting non-Indian origins.

Essential reading for understanding Buddhist thought origins include Dr. Ranajit Pal's ("The Dawn of Religions in **Afghanistan**-Seistan-Gandhara, 2000)" (**Pal**, 2000)[5]; Harvey Craft's "The Buddha from Babylon" (**Kraft**, 2014)[6], and Christopher Beckwith's "The Greek Buddha" , Pyrrho's Encounter with Early Buddhism in Central Asia) (Beckwith, 2017)[7].

---

5. Pal, D. R. (2000). "The Dawn of Religions in Afghanistan-Seistan-Gandhara.

6. Kraft, H. (2014). The Buddha From Babylon. Select Books

7. Beckwith, C. (2017). The Greek Buddha. Princeton Universty Press.

Behistun Inscription Reliefs.

The Behistun Inscription is a multilingual Achaemenid royal inscription and a large rock relief. It was produced during the reign of Darius I the Great (r. 522–486 BC).

Further scholarly works listed in the footnotes offer invaluable insights into Siddhartha Gautama's historical antecedents.[8,9,10,11]

✹ ✹ ✹

Siddhartha's pacifist calls starkly contrasted the brutal era marked by power-hungry kings and warlords. People, ever ready to flee or face

---

8.   Ancient Persian Inscriptions Link a Babylonian King to the Man Who Became Buddha | Ancient Origins (ancient-origins.net)

9.   Okar Research: Ilkhanid Buddhism & Eurasian Iran (1256-1335 AD) (balkhandshambhala.blogspot.com)

10.   10 Kamālashraī - Rashaīd al-daīn's "life and teaching of Buddha". A source for the Buddhism of the Mongol period on jstor.

11.   Behistun Inscription - Wikipedia

obliteration, sought solace in his empowering message amid ceaseless warfare and ruthless games of thrones.

Another reason the Buddha's teachings thrived, was that it was seen to counter an entrenched Vedic religion, held captive by power-hungry priests and an autocratic sway over the laity.

It may be useful to understand the enigmatic origins and the sources of power that bolstered the priestly classes. Before their grip on the sacred realms tightened, there were primordial shaman-seers that roamed freely, delving into the unseen by tapping into the transcendent faculties of the super-conscious mind. They achieved this feat by dismantling the barriers between the Conscious and the Unconscious, thereby unveiling the mysteries and hidden laws embedded in life itself.

These secrets of shamans were an unveiling the superconscious states heralding a pivotal moment in human history; marking the transition from a life governed by instinct to one propelled by intellectual pursuits, such as philosophy. The ineffable experiences of the ancients, once documented, crystallized into canonical wisdom, shaping the course of culture and civilization.

This divine authority that once resided in the shaman of a tribe, bereft of any institutionalized structure, gradually shifted to the ruling body of a priesthood. This new power centre assumed guardianship over sacred spaces and practices, forging a hierarchical structure that mirrored the celestial order of the gods and their retinues. High priests, specialty priests, god-servants, and caretakers formed an intricate chain of command that simultaneously served as a social model, delineating clear strata among royal, warrior, commercial, and social organizations.

Armed with absolute power, the clergy wielded their influence to demand tributes and sacrifices, appeasing the insatiable hunger of the gods. They admonished the masses, warning that failure to satisfy the divine beings would unleash chaos and summon malevolent spirits into the world, spelling potential doom in the afterlife.

While this exclusive cabal of priests reaped the benefits of their elevated status, it must be acknowledged that their dominion laid the foundation for the community and fostered an ordered society. Bound by a strict code of rules and regulations, this structure created a framework for the flourishing of civilizations and the cultivation of human potential. This burgeoning stratification in society evolved into a caste-based hierarchy, delineating those with privileged access to the Divine from those without[12]. This division instituted a set of rules that, once adhered to, established a protocol between the upper and lower castes. Theology and dogma became a tool to instill both fear and order; perceived misdeeds, as judged by these gatekeepers, would yield dire consequences, making obedience and compliance imperative.

When a lower caste individual sought a bountiful harvest or a merchant aspired for success in trade, they would consult their local priest, who would in turn consult the Vedas and prescribe intricate rituals. The efficacy of these rites was rarely scrutinized; yet, whether these practices contributed to the ultimate goal of Liberation or *Moksha* remained equally uncertain. As **Friedrich Nietzsche** astutely observed, before one can sell the notion of 'Redemption' through religion, it is essential to first convince people of their need for it.

This proto-fascist ideology required a blind acceptance of these practices and authority was the sole means of ensuring that the soul fulfilled its righteous duties. Deviation from this path risked rebirth in a degraded state, jeopardizing the prospect of *Moksha*. For centuries preceding the advent of the Buddha, this dogma held sway over the lives of those residing in the Gangetic plain.

This intricate web of rules, regulations, and structures designed for the soul's liberation was meticulously codified in Vedic literature. Known as the Dharmic system, it remains synonymous with the *'Right Hand of God'*. This ancient framework, entrenched in the social fabric, has persisted through the ages, reflecting the enduring influence of these early stratifications and the potency of religious authority.

---

12. "Buddhism and Cast" by Y. Krishnan (JSTOR, 1969)

Around this time, other branches of spirituality were sprouting, and individuals were accessing "Divine" powers through their personal practices, challenging the priestly class. These challenges came from the rise of asceticism, scepticism, practices of Yoga and Meditation, and other forms of non-Brahmanical practices referred to as Tantra or the *'Left Hand of God'*. Tantric practices by wandering ascetics became the alternative for those who opposed the strict orthodoxy and regulations of Brahmanism. It was through their practices of asceticism, scepticism, and a growing mercantile class as the new sponsors of these ascetics, that the new teachings of the Buddha began to spread and gain traction among the laity.

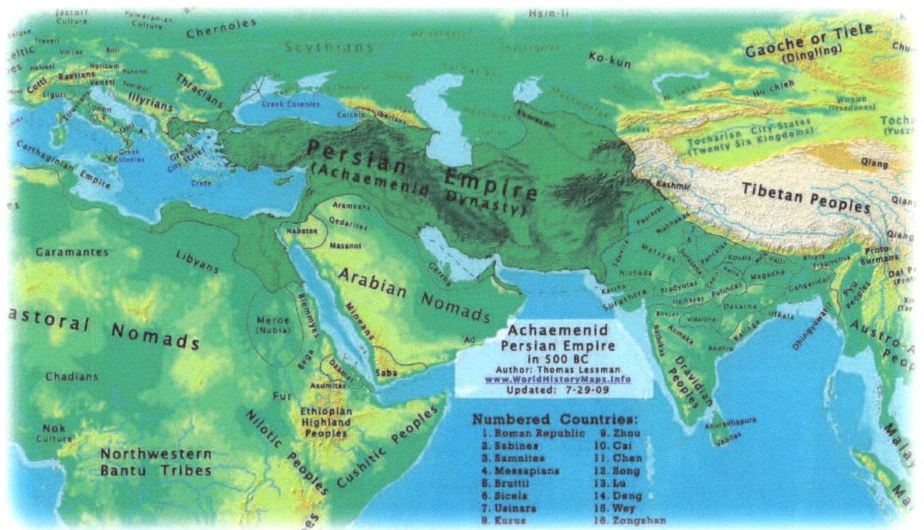

Map of Kingdoms 500 BC

Building upon the insights of the Greeks and the Zoroastrians, the Buddha presented a cohesive vision of existence as seen from the grand perch of his enlightened Universal-Mind. He proposed that all human beings could access the same divine forces directly, circumventing the powerful priestly class and setting the stage for a democratic and universal spirituality. This was not Buddhism as we know it today, but rather the earliest Buddhist period of doubt and scepticism against the orthodoxy of the day.

If the Buddha and his followers needed to educate the people on this new teaching, they had to proselytize to free the masses from spiritual exclusion. This is where the earliest Buddhist teachings came into their own. Instead of competing with other religions like Brahmanism, Zoroastrianism, or Jainism, the Buddha simply removed god from the equation and put the focus back on the individual.

Here was born a new atheistic religiosity.

The essence of Buddha's teachings was to tear down the veils that had been meticulously constructed by the guardians of orthodoxy, who steadfastly insisted that their path was the exclusive route to *Moksha* or spiritual liberation.

The Buddha's approach offered an alternative that challenged these conventional gatekeepers, suggesting that the attainment of enlightenment was accessible to all. By revealing the mechanisms behind the so-called magic rituals, the Buddha encouraged individuals to question the very existence of the mystical aspects that had previously been associated with '*Moksha*'.

By demystifying the path to enlightenment, the Buddha's teachings emphasized the importance of personal experience and self-discovery. This approach fostered a sense of empowerment, as individuals were no longer reliant on the dictates of orthodox gatekeepers to navigate their spiritual journey. Instead, they were encouraged to cultivate introspection, allowing them to pierce through the veil of illusion and grasp the true nature of reality.

The Buddha's teachings heralded a pioneering shift towards self-governance, resembling an early form of spiritual democracy. This transformative approach liberated individuals from dependence on divine dictatorships and the constraints of orthodox practices, granting them the autonomy to seek their own way out of the cycle of suffering.

His teachings underscored that it was not necessary to depend on divine intervention or engage in intricate rites and rituals to attain Nirvana. Rather, individuals from all walks of life could achieve this transcendent state if they sincerely adhered to the Four Noble Truths[13] and the Eightfold Path[14], regardless of their social standing or caste.

This radical shift in perspective empowered people to take control of their own spiritual journey, fostering a sense of personal responsibility and accountability. By emphasizing the importance of mindfulness and ethical conduct, the Buddha's teachings provided a clear and accessible path for individuals to chart their own course toward liberation.

The stage was now set for the emergence of a novel literary genre of spiritual texts, which would proliferate and foster a culture of proselytization, ultimately loosening the grip of the dominant clergy on the masses. These transformative texts, such as the Diamond Sutra, would be read, copied *en masse*, and disseminated among the laity, who had previously been denied access to sacred scriptures like the Vedas.

This paradigm shift not only ushered in a new epoch in spiritual literature but also refocused attention on the individual. The empowerment drawn from scepticism and a straightforward commitment to ethics, which offered the promise of eternal life, motivated individuals to liberate themselves from the constraints of hierarchical structures. It inspired them to embark on personal journeys of self-discovery, introspection, and development. Crucially, this shift set the stage for individuals to question humanity's position in the universe and explore the concept of a unique Self or Personhood.

Here, we witness the initial endeavours of our ancient forebears, who composed transformative texts such as the Diamond Sutra, which would significantly alter the spiritual landscape. As these profound manuscripts disseminated rapidly, they promised a more inclusive and accessible path to enlightenment for all who earnestly pursued it.

---

13. Four Noble Truths: Dukka, (suffering); Samudaya (origin of Suffering); Nirodha (Understanding of Suffering); Magga (Path to end suffering)

14. Noble Eightfold Path - Wikipedia

Just as our forebears responded to the questions of the laity regarding our place in the Universe, in today's modern landscape of Artificial Intelligence, concepts such as the Self or Non-Self have been thrust into sharper focus. Intriguingly, our own creations and our place within this emerging non-organic intelligence are now challenging humanity's position and heightening our anxiety regarding our Identity and our place within the Universe. This drastic shift has unwittingly led us to a situation where we've allowed our sense of authority and authenticity to be eroded.

As we venture into the following chapters, I invite you to join me on a journey of exploration. Together, we will explore our gradual shift from an uncritical dependence on sacred texts that guide our lives, to an analogous reverence and acceptance of Artificial Intelligence as a silicon deity.

I see this not only as a technological issue but also as a deeply existential one of our own making- it represents the core crisis we face today.

Chapter 2

The Four Most Important Words. (Verse 1)

VERSE 1 THE CONVOCATION OF THE ASSEMBLY

Thus, have I heard.

Upon a time Buddha sojourned in Anathapindika's Park by Shravasti with a great company of bhikshus, even twelve hundred and fifty. One day, at the time for breaking fast, the World-honoured One enrobed, and carrying His bowl made His way into the great city of Shravasti to beg for His food. In the midst of the city He begged from door to door according to rule. This done, He returned to His retreat and took His meal. When He had finished He put away His robe and begging bowl, washed His feet, arranged His seat, and sat down.

"Thus, have I heard"

The Diamond Sutra unfurls with these words that, while seemingly simple, carry great depth and wisdom, placing them among the most significant words, across spiritual texts worldwide.

Often, scholars focus on the complexities of philosophy and sadly overlook these opening lines, which offer valuable guidance for spiritual seekers from various traditions and cultures.

The first four words of the Diamond Sutra have been cherished for centuries, as they provide both the speaker and listener with a clear direction for navigating the world of subjective experience. At first glance, they may appear to distance the speaker from the words of another, but their true essence lies in recognizing the unique and indescribable nature of subjective experiences.

Unlike scientific subjects that can be measured and defined objectively, subjective experiences cannot be translated into a common language or a consensus reality. These opening words warn against the pitfalls of language and reification, suggesting they can serve as a warning for interpreting the more enigmatic verses of the Diamond Sutra that follow.

Unfortunately, throughout history, preachers and scholars have mistakenly believed that their interpretations of spiritual texts could reflect absolute truths in a common language. This misconception led to the distortion of words, rather than understanding the seeker's or the person's subjective mental phenomena and indescribable experience. As we know, everyone's private world is a vibrant landscape of unique experiences that give rise to personal insights and revelations that cannot be duplicated.

Hence, the speakers who expound on another's experience or texts such as these say, *"Thus, have I heard."*

When we look at a captivating painting, it is not just the colours and shapes that hold our attention; it is the essence of the artist that breathes life into each stroke and curve. In that moment of contemplation, both the viewer and the creator become fully present, each dwelling in their distinct experiences. However, the crux of the matter lies in the fact that these individual perspectives are deeply personal and subjective, any attempts to combine them into a shared language or reality is impossible.

By focusing on their own Direct Experiences, rather than relying on hearsay or external authority, or texts, seekers can explore the depths of their authentic truth, moving beyond speculation and inference. Spiritual texts become secondary in the presence of such direct experience. Without engaging in the inner world of phenomena that leads to authentic experience, spiritual texts are merely illusions of knowledge, even irrelevant.

Once again, I encourage the discerning reader to reflect on the significance of the Sutra's opening verse.

This opening verse's introduction, with its distinctive literary style compared to the remaining verses, hints at a different penmanship to the rest of the Diamond Sutra-. It provides a fleeting glimpse into the writer's autonomy.

The writer of this opening verse presents a modest image of the Buddha engaging in everyday mundane tasks, an infrequently mentioned depiction that highlights his grounded nature as an ordinary man immersed in daily life. This insightful portrayal demonstrates the Buddha's commitment to living fully in the present moment, embracing life's richness and the interconnected world, rather than constantly striving to attain Buddhahood in isolation.

Ironically, this depiction suggests that the path to Buddhahood lies not in relentless pursuit but in being completely immersed in the present moment.- which is our first-hand experience. This message is delivered with straightforward simplicity, implying that by ceasing to strive, the path to enlightenment will reveal itself, and to achieve Buddhahood, one must let go of the desire to become a Buddha.

And with that opening message, we are left to reflect on the implications of this introduction. If one does not fully appreciate the deeper meaning of these four words, recognizing that direct experience is the only true reality, the rest of the Diamond Sutra might merely be seen as inspiring prose.

Chapter 3

Meet Your Artificial Self - (Verses 2, 3)

VERSE 2; SUBHUTI MAKES A REQUEST

Now in the midst of the assembly was the Venerable Subhuti. Forthwith he arose, uncovered his right shoulder, knelt upon his right knee, and, respectfully raising his hands with palms joined, addressed the Buddha thus: Wonderful World-honoured One, in the case of a son or daughter of a good family, or good men and good women who seek the Consummation of Incomparable Enlightenment, by what criteria should they abide and how should they control their thoughts?

Buddha said:

Very good, Subhuti! Just as you say, the Tathagata is ever-mindful of all the Bodhisattvas, protecting and instructing them well. Now listen and take my words to heart: I will declare to you by what criteria good men and good women seeking the Consummation of Incomparable Enlightenment should abide, and how they should control their thoughts. Said Subhuti: Pray, do, World-honoured One. With joyful anticipation we long to hear.

It's like the authors didn't even realize the hidden gem tucked away in the opening verse, because, from here on, the narrative takes on a different penmanship, hurtling into a universe of daring speculations and profound metaphysical musings.

The Venerable Subhuti now raises a question about how children from noble families or virtuous men and women seeking the "Consummation of Incomparable Enlightenment" can attain such a state.

This selfish inquiry about the path to enlightenment raises an important question: Did the early followers believe that the Buddha's teachings were to be accessible to everyone, regardless of their background? Did they accept enlightenment was reserved exclusively for the privileged and upper castes?

The term "Good Son or Daughter" is a direct translation from the Sanskrit "*Kula Putra*," which reveals the culture of the earliest Buddhist converts were influenced by their culture of Brahmanism, who continued their earlier dogma of curtailed direct access to the Divine to the lower castes.

In the nascent days of Buddhism, these sagacious "*Djiva*"[15] - the twice-born elite - were its first disciples. Hailing from an insular, priestly caste, they clung to dogma at odds with the Buddha's egalitarian message. Even as they embraced the "new" teachings, the lingering vestiges of their caste-bound past, refused to be shaken off.

Even though the practice of religious exclusion remains prevalent even today, Buddhism initially found acceptance in the subcontinent through the conversion and patronage of royalty, such as Emperor Ashoka[16]. Centuries later, Hinduism had a resurgence, but Buddhism had already spread outside the subcontinent, to countries where Hinduism did not find widespread acceptance in the first place[17].

In response to Subhuti's question, the Buddha continues,

VERSE 3 THE REAL TEACHING OF THE GREAT WAY

Buddha said: Subhuti, all the Bodhisattva-Heroes should discipline their thoughts as follows: All living creatures of

---

15.   Dvija - Wikipedia

16.   Why Did Ashoka Convert to Buddhism - DailyHistory.org

17.   Buddhism - The demise of Buddhism in India | Britannica

whatever class, born from eggs, from wombs, from moisture, or by transformation whether with form or without form, whether in a state of thinking or exempt from thought-necessity, or wholly beyond all thought realms, all these are caused by Me to attain Unbounded Liberation Nirvana.

The second part of the verse paradoxically recognizes that there is no need for liberation since our original state is indivisible from the Other, Source, or Tathagata, thus rendering effort unnecessary. Sentiments echoed by the 17th-century Jewish-Dutch philosopher **Benedict de Spinoza** who said " Without God, nothing can be nor be conceived, *but that all things are in God. Wherefore nothing can exist, outside Himself….*".

If there is no separation between you, me, and all of us, then there is no Buddha above or below us. It would be extremely egotistical to declare, "Caused by Me" and expect the entire universe to be led toward Nirvana by a single individual. These three words have elevated Siddhartha Gautama to the status of a god, contrary to his teachings. Perhaps we should contemplate that this word has been grossly mistranslated, and "Me", means "The Highest Self."

In the Christian Bible, the word is similarly corrupted: "No man cometh to the Father, except through Me!" Replace "Me" with "The Highest Self," that Spirit that is intrinsically entwined with the Cosmos or Universal Consciousness, and yet purposefully unique: To attain Oneness with the Father, we need only embrace our innate unity with the Universe. Our divine amnesia has a purpose, but the Buddha speaks unambiguously – paraphrasing this verse - "We are already perfect, and striving for perfection is a futile endeavour."

THE BUDDHA'S RESPONSE READS:

"Yet when vast, uncountable, immeasurable numbers of beings have thus been liberated, verily no being has been liberated. Why is this, Subhuti? It is because no Bodhisattva who is a real Bodhisattva cherishes the idea of an ego-entity, a personality, a being, or a separated individuality."

The Buddha's response is particularly pertinent as our contemporary minds grapple with the diversity of nature and our place in it.

One could ask: if non-duality or non-separation is our 'true' state, why is it that the cosmos unfurls as a kaleidoscope of discrete beings, exploding outwards from the first dawn of time, or, as physicists refer to that moment as Singularity? Why is there a need for evolution and expansion? Why is there a need for such diversity in the Universe?

These questions, inherently anthropocentric, should prompt us to venture beyond our human framework, striving to grasp a universal perspective that may transcend our confines of space and time. For instance, consider Earth's history before humans existed when dinosaurs and other mysterious creatures dominated the landscape. Humans are a late entrant in the evolutionary arc; but before we appeared, what was the role of Universal Consciousness when dinosaurs and extinct creatures inhabited the Earth, and asteroids bombarded the planet regularly before humans began to pose this question?

Presently, we share our planet with organisms like cockroaches and innumerable viruses, which contribute to the spread of numerous diseases and cause widespread suffering. What is the need for these creatures in this expanse of diversity? Such questions arise from the human-centric hubris of our self-anointed dominance in the diversity of consciousness.

While our perspective is limited to the diversity found on our planet, it is not unreasonable to consider the possibility that within the vast reaches of space, filled with billions of galaxies, there may be other life forms beyond our current understanding.

Indeed, life as we know it is a small part of the grand tapestry of the cosmos. Recognizing our tiny role in the cosmic theatre should inspire a sense of humility, especially if we consider the possibility that if the Universe was to experience a hypothetical disturbance, all life could vanish, and the cosmos would continue its path, impervious to our brief presence.

This Cosmic indifference is not too hard to imagine as the Cosmos displays the destructive forces found throughout the universe: exploding supernovas, and black holes consuming entire galaxies. Chaos and violence seem to be the default state of the cosmos. It is reasonable to assume that our planet, our solar system, and our Galaxy, the Milky Way will eventually meet the same fate.

Faced with such overwhelming forces, we must ask ourselves: what should be the State of human Consciousness if everything we are attached to, our beliefs, and all that we consider sacred were to disappear into nothingness? It might not take billions of years for this to happen; a catastrophic asteroid impact or a nuclear disaster could wipe out life on Earth, erasing our civilization and everything we hold sacred.

In this scenario of an extinction event like the dinosaurs, we are compelled to question the purpose of evolutionary biology, because seemingly, the *intent* of the Universe was one of *Duality and Diversity*. What, then, is the true nature and purpose of our seemingly insignificant existence in this expanse of the Universe?

Instead of asking questions within questions or pondering the imponderable, like "Who am I", perhaps it may be simpler to start with "Why am I here"? What do I need to do in this incarnation? How can I give meaning and purpose to my life"?

These are some of the questions that pierce the core of our shared human journey, as we attempt to unravel our Self and our essence amidst the diversity of consciousness that we call Life. It is only through these encounters and interactions with the Other, be they people or objects, that cultivates our subjective understanding of the world and our appreciation of the essence of our Personhood.

Even amid the copious diversity of our world, the riddle of the Self has been fervently debated. The Buddha posits that our Self is either non-existent entirely or dissolved within the intricate interdependence of the manifested Universe. The concepts of life's interdependence and the notion of "non-self" or "no-self," depending on one's perspective, give rise to a fundamental question: *how do we demarcate our humanity and distinguish our individuality from the collective consciousness?*

Regrettably, such convictions of 'non-self' or 'no self' have conditioned us to equate lesser forms of consciousness with human consciousness.

I am open to correction if I've misinterpreted this verse, but I must emphasize that the sublimation and non-recognition of our sovereignty over other life forms have impeded our understanding of our sense of Selfhood and our relationship with the manifested Universe. In my view, the second part of this Verse reveals a doctrine that unapologetically equates human awareness to lesser beings and inanimate entities and challenges the sovereignty of human awareness.

I must clarify that I am not advocating for humans to assert complete dominion over the biosphere. As advanced cognitive beings, we have a responsibility for the Earth's stewardship, protecting our planet against ecocide. However, the millennia-old doctrine equating all things to the human level has emboldened theocratic governments to elevate even non-animate objects to the level of human awareness and consciousness.

Alarmingly, some South Asian governments have issued ID cards to rivers, mountains, and rocks, bestowing equal legal rights to us humans. But if the Self is non-existent or submerged within the ecosphere, how can we unveil our Personhood? What constitutes our sense of being? Our human state? What enables us to assert, "This is me, and importantly, that is not me?" Undoubtedly, your cat purring on your sofa or your dog has an inner theatre, giving it a sense of "I am Milo, a cat," or "I am Rufus, a dog." What is it to be a cat or dog, distinct from their human caretakers? Can a school of dolphins switch to being human automatically, 'on porpoise'? I hope you won't consider me trying to be flippant; the point is we should accept that our sense of identity should be self-evident. Only you can confirm that you are who you are and what and how you feel when you look at yourself in the mirror. *Why is that so*?

Millennia of social and religious conditioning have promoted a false equivalence between lower consciousness and human beings, and by extension, among all life forms. These deep-seated beliefs have predisposed us to acknowledge the dominance of humanity's latest creation - Artificial Intelligence. Alarmingly, we are now accepting these bits of artificial intelligence not just as equals, but as some are claiming AI *is even superior to humankind!*

This is where the rubber meets the road for me, and I hope to exfoliate some of these conundrums in subsequent chapters.

Humanity's surrender of our sovereignty to an external authority and even our own creation like Artificial Intelligence presents the most pressing crisis that the world faces today. News columns are replete with pundits wondering if the next version of AI will replace humans in 10 years!

Ironically, we now also acknowledge the tremendous challenges presented by the asymmetry of nature and its capacity for the unlimited display of force.

We now firmly believe that our survival as a species hinges on utilizing and mastering technology so that we may evolve into Human+(Plus), an Avatar of ourselves, to transcend our human limitations.

By relegating human consciousness to the narrow confines of what can be measured, categorized, and quantified, we have succumbed to the disquieting consensus that humanity can *only* be measured.

By *measuring* nature, we convince ourselves that we can *control* it. Consequently, we have relinquished our sense of Personhood to blend into this vision of a mechanized world. In our current era, this manifestation of a mechanized and industrial age manifests as the cybernetic Metaverse, governed by artificial intelligence that we now regard as superior to our own.

Progress is now seen as a submission to a TechnoUtopia, where the promise of a perfect world and augmented humans has come at a great cost to our individuality.

Our creations, such as Artificial Intelligence and Robotics, are now considered more real and superior to us in every way, and even children are coerced into learning coding languages at a young age to serve as mere coding coolies in the cybernetic network.

Decades ago, power lay with those who controlled access to the oil, but today data has taken its place as the new oil. Power now lies where data is captured and stored as we move into the surveillance economy where you and I are the data points.

Startups, once born in garages and dorm rooms, have redrawn the world map, establishing economic boundaries. These entities, including Facebook, Google, Apple, Amazon, Alibaba, and Weibo, earn more than the GDP of many nations, prompting governments to feel threatened by their dominance and will try to regulate them and seize control of the data. Multinational companies operating in China are forced to keep all their data inland and hand it over when demanded. With the data of every Chinese citizen, the AI engine can monitor and control an entire population. The tanks of Tiananmen Square have been replaced by smartphones and apps like TikTok and Weibo whose AI engines guide its citizens into compliance without its citizenry aware of that surveillance and manipulation. In this brave new world, computers have assumed the authority to decide our humanity.

Our readiness to embrace AI arises not only from its sheer power but tragically also from our surrender of individuality. This stems from our incapacity for original and critical thought as an opposition to this nonorganic intelligence. We have relinquished our higher consciousness and human abilities to a digitized Avatar we hold in reverence.

We convince ourselves that consensus opinion has become the new intelligence, and we've chosen this collective belief over our innate creativity and critical thinking. In doing so, we willingly sacrifice our selfhood to cybernetic groupthink, allowing the AI machine and its controllers to dominate.

The cybernetic TechnoUtopia fuelled by Artificial Intelligence is, ultimately, the epitome of Group Think.

Like the venerated external sources and sutras that falsely equate human consciousness with lesser entities, we continue to relinquish our sovereignty and authority to anything with a semblance of Artificial Intelligence that displays false human sentience.

For millennia, we have blindly venerated external sources, demonstrating the surrender of our authority to doctrines that diminish our human consciousness. *Today's computer languages bear an uncanny resemblance to religious canons, to which we pay homage.*

I maintain, that Artificial Intelligence will continue to play a dominant role in our lives. The challenge lies in striking a balance between embracing our uniquely human qualities and harnessing the power of technology for our betterment. By doing so, we can strive to maintain our identity as human beings while evolving into a more resilient, adaptable, and interconnected species.

Chapter 4

Stairway to Heaven, The Buddha's Version (Verses 4, 5)

VERSE 4: EVEN THE MOST BENEFICENT PRACTICES ARE RELATIVE

Furthermore, Subhuti, in the practice of charity a Bodhisattva should be detached. That is to say, he should practice charity without regard to appearances; without regard to sound, odour, touch, flavor or any thought that arises in it. Subhuti, thus should the Bodhisattva practice charity without being supported by any notion of a sign. Wherefore? In such a case his merit is incalculable. Subhuti, what do you think? Can you measure all the space extending eastward? No, World-honoured One, I cannot. Then can you, Subhuti, measure all the space extending southward, westward, northward, or in any other direction, including nadir and zenith? No, World-honoured One, I cannot. Well, Subhuti, equally incalculable is the merit of the Bodhisattva who practices charity without any attachment to appearances. Subhuti, Bodhisattvas should persevere one-pointedly in this instruction.

[Subhuti, thus should the Bodhisattva practice charity without attachment].

Buddha pioneered an unprecedented model of spiritual democratization, transferring authority from the clergy to the individual. This transformation was embodied in a personally tailored journey towards Nirvana, underscored by moral conduct. While this philosophy wasn't entirely innovative, it was significantly refined by Buddha and his disciples. Their strong advocacy of consistent ethical practice offered a path to heightened spiritual power and mystical experiences, facets rarely discussed in previous religions.

PART (I): THE FOCUS ON ETHICS.

The Sutra begins with two verses that focus on ethics. These verses set the tone for the rest of the text, which emphasizes the importance of living a moral and ethical life as a way of reaching Nirvana. The theme of ethics is recursive throughout the Sutra, and it is one of the central teachings of Buddhism. Readers would find it beneficial to revisit these passages when later verses recite the theme of ethical practice and "signage" or "marks" on the body as evidence of progress on the spiritual path.

The verse's core tenet, *"your act should be unsupported by any sign,"* calls for ethical actions free from expectation, a theme present in many religions, such as Zoroastrianism and Christianity.

Zoroastrianism's moral order includes virtues like Wisdom and Charity, echoing the six ethics in the Diamond Sutra, which share similarities with Greek philosophies from a millennium prior. The Diamond Sutra regards the ethic of generosity or '*Dana*" as the highest act of righteousness, incorporating all other perfections. This parallels the New Testament's story "The Widow's Offering' in the Book of Mark 12:41-44, as an example of non-attachment.

The Verse's use of "Signs" refers to stains of expectation, and "signless" means having no investment in the outcome of charity. However, Subhuti says the merit of generosity is unfathomable and immeasurable, emphasizing ethics as a means of achieving enlightenment.

Once, when I was accompanied by a devout Buddhist we observed monks and devotees participating in acts of Dana[18]. The monks were seated cross-legged on stools, clothed in burgundy and ochre robes with fake Rolexes dangling on their wrists, impressively impassive with

---

18.   Pali: PindaPatta

their begging bowls[19] in front of them. Both the devotees and the monks seemed to have their own agenda by their acts of *Dana*. The question that arose between us as we watched was: Who was more stained, the exploitative monks or the merit-seeking devotees?

We agreed that practicing ethics with a pure heart leads to a deeper interconnectedness of all beings. This non-attachment to outcomes, combined with sincere ethical practice, forms the foundation for an authentic spiritual journey in the pursuit of Buddha nature.

VERSE 5: UNDERSTANDING THE ULTIMATE PRINCIPLE OF REALITY

Subhuti, what do you think? Is the Tathagata to be recognized by some bodily marks? No, World honoured One; the Tathagata cannot be recognized by any bodily marks.

Wherefore? Because the Tathagata has said that material characteristics are not, in fact, material characteristics. Buddha said: Subhuti, wheresoever are material characteristics there is delusion; but who so perceives that all characteristics are in fact no-characteristics, perceives the Tathagata.

PART (II): ACHIEVING SIGNS, PSYCHIC BODIES BY ETHICS

[The Diamond Sutra's inclusion of this dry and abstract section is not the focus of my commentary.

This verse alludes to the psychic anatomy that advanced practitioners attain as a sign of their progress, such as the **Arahat** *and* **Anuttara Samyak Sambodhi** *states[20]. These signs or marks represent the attainment of the absolute Buddha nature, but debates have raged for millennia over their true meaning and necessity.*

While this section of the chapter may come across as somewhat arcane and theological, it's essential to pause and pay heed to this passage.

---

19. Pali: Patta; Sankskrit: Patra

20. Anuttara-samyak-sambodhi - Tibetan Buddhist Encyclopedia

The original authors of the Diamond Sutra ingeniously interweave ontological elements into ethical practices. In this context, physical manifestations become indicators of enlightenment, enduring across multiple lifetimes.

*The reader can jump to **part (iii) 'Are we there yet'** within this chapter if they wish.]*

In the following paragraphs, I aim to elaborate on one of the propositions put forth throughout this book regarding spiritual effort and practices. Rather than striving for these esoteric states, I question why one should strive to become something they are not, instead of being present in the moment.

The quest towards 'enlightenment' like Arahat often lures us into thinking it can be reached through well-defined paths or systems, such as certain meditative practices or disciplined practices of ethics.

However, this mindset is flawed as we are required to aspire to and focus on altered states that are beyond our conceptual grasp, which is as elusive as meditating on a pot of gold at the end of a rainbow.

Instead of locking in the mind to fit into a specific pattern, no matter how attractive, the true need is to unchain the mind, allowing it to freely explore and discover.

The more dynamic and rewarding path for understanding our own consciousness is by observing, reflecting, and learning from the diverse phenomena that we encounter in our lives. A lived experience provides insight and meaning into the nature of our own consciousness.

The verse from the **Shurangama Sutra**, which I introduced in the chapter concerning the history of the Buddha, takes on a renewed significance when viewed through this lens. Its profound wisdom is not merely a philosophical musing, but also an insightful observation about the way the human mind can be trained to expand.

Recalling that Sutra:

"It is said, Dharma does not arise alone. Relying on conditions it is born. The Way is not practiced in vain. Meeting conditions, there is a response".,

This verse hints at the dynamic nature of cultures and civilizations, reacting and adapting to the prevalent circumstances, perpetually evolving. However, its implications are not just collective but also personal. For the individual, it suggests how we, as individuals, can learn to understand our responses to phenomena that occur in our lives, how we can adapt, and ultimately, how we can evolve by incremental insight. Only contextual experience can give true learning and meaning to Life.

The verse from the Shurangama Sutra provides a sharper lens through which we can view the forthcoming discussion, enriching our understanding and comprehension, and illuminating a way for us to navigate our lives more consciously.

Incidentally, this Verse 5 contrasts with the opening verse, which if you recall claims no effort is needed. This verse refers to signs on the body, alluding to subtler bodies as hallmarks of a practitioner's achievements.

In the early Buddhist tradition, Buddhahood is recognized through acquiring 32 bodily marks[21] and the ten powers of **Anuttara Samyak Sambodi**. Subhuti argues that these marks pertain to the physical body, not the **Dharmakāya** body. The 32 marks originate from the **Avadana** philosophy, which emphasizes personal effort across lifetimes for salvation. A central tension arises from the preoccupation with these marks, contrasting with the Arhat who lacks them.

The Buddha asserts that even attaining the Trikaya bodies[22] cannot serve as a sign or form in the Dharmakaya body[23], as Emptiness (Shunyata) constitutes true Buddha nature. This concept of signs through diligent ethical practice proposes a universal ontology for spiritual attainment.

---

21.   Physical characteristics of the Buddha - Wikipedia

22.   Trikaya - Wikipedia

23.   Dharmakaya, or "truth body," is one of the three bodies of a Buddha according to the Trikaya doctrine in Mahayana Buddhism.

These goals or waypoints that are highlighted in this text raise the question of whether it is possible to discuss, speculate or aspire to any state without experiencing it first. Further, are all seekers required to achieve and display these marks like waypoints on the path?

The preoccupation with signs and marks derived through diligent ethical practice perplexed scholars, as it contradicted the Buddha's proclamation that all form is unreal.

If you have travelled in Asia, you may notice an irony with those who adorn themselves with religious symbols, *malas,* and particular dress codes It raises questions about the sincerity of those who display marks and trappings of religiosity while overlooking the resilience and struggle inherent in simpler expressions of spirituality.

These two verses highlight this tension between the pursuit of enlightenment and the preoccupation with signs, marks, and external symbols. This preoccupation can detract from the true nature of spiritual growth and realization, which is rooted in personal experience and internal transformation.

The pursuit of enlightenment should focus on the cultivation of inner qualities, such as wisdom, compassion, and self-awareness, rather than on external symbols or marks of attainment. If harmony is achieved in our inner world, no cosmetic dress or advertisement would be needed!

The **Yogacharya school** introduced the concept of "Alayavijnana," or the "Body of Consciousness," as a response to the emphasis on the 32 physical signs of Buddhahood. This purported psychic anatomy extends beyond the physical, and is also known as the **Tathagatagarbha** or the "Womb of the Tathagata."

The goal of Tathagatagarbha, a disembodied state of non-knowing or nothingness, analogously known as the "Alayavijnana," is a foundational concept in some schools of Buddhism, represents the "storehouse consciousness" where all potential experiences and knowledge exist, ready to manifest in another place and time.

Modern interpreters and scholars have devoted considerable effort to drawing poetic comparisons between the concept of "Alayavijnana" and the quantum field theory, finding intriguing intersections that somehow confirm their conjectures towards an overarching understanding of reality[24]. (*More of this later*)

Quantum Field Theory (QFT), a fundamental framework in physics, also resonates with similar notions. It describes a universe where every particle is an excitation of an underlying field that exists everywhere and at all times, hinting at a boundless potentiality that can give rise to particles and forces at any point in space and time.

The perceived congruence between these two concepts is not merely a matter of curiosity but a potent source of philosophical and scientific conjecture. Both "Alayavijnana" and the QFT embrace the idea that matter and consciousness could potentially enfold and then manifest in different places and times, suggesting a universe brimming with untapped potential and interconnectedness.

Adding an even more forward-thinking perspective to this discussion is the rapidly evolving field of Artificial Intelligence (AI) and its implications for the Metaverse. The Metaverse, an envisioned collective virtual shared space, created by the convergence of virtually enhanced physical reality and physically persistent virtual reality, promises unprecedented advancements in AI. These advancements could offer insights into the creation of conscious systems and the dynamics of information and cognition that might echo and expand upon the insights provided by the "Alayavijnana" concept and quantum field theory.

The parallels drawn between these vastly different concepts are not only remarkable for their imaginative and creative license but also for their potential to illuminate new pathways in our understanding of

---

24. Towards reconstruction of the dialogue between Modern Physics and Buddhist Philosophy: an inquiry into the concepts of Quantum Vacuum and Ālayavijñāna (researchgate.net)

consciousness, reality, and the digital worlds we are increasingly weaving into the fabric of human experience.

However, back on Planet Earth, we should be more concerned by the Buddha's assertion that *"all with form is not real"* which prompts us to scrutinize the very nature of reality and the personal experience of selfhood, especially considering the emerging era of AI. This dualistic perspective resonates with **Adi Shankara's**[25] philosophy asserting that *"all is Illusion, and there is only the Absolute or Brahma."*

Such a blanket statement invites us to question our own existence: Are we, indeed, not real? Is our perception of the 'Self' not self-evident? Or is it merely a complex illusion presented by our minds? When I look into a mirror, I know it is me. How do I know this? That which is self-evident needs no proof! Such lines of questioning grows increasingly relevant as we approach a future where artificial entities may seem to possess their own semblance of consciousness and identity.

This philosophical musing also raises important questions about the path of spiritual development. If all is an illusion except the absolute, what does it mean for the practices of ethical acts and spiritual disciplines performed over countless lifetimes to attain enlightenment? Should we just sit on our thumbs and do nothing about climate change? Is it necessary to follow a linear trajectory towards enlightenment, or could insight act as a catalyst, enabling us to leapfrog to our highest potential selves, bypassing intermediary stages?

Furthermore, the illusory objective of focusing on psychic bodies and other esoteric states could potentially distract spiritual seekers from focusing on their immediate, subjective experiences.

It is vital to acknowledge that these esoteric states, do not exist in the present existential moment. Our focus should be centred on the here and now, as dwelling on anything outside this moment and beyond our direct experience is an illusion, at best mere conjecture.

---

25. *Ādi Śhaṅkara*, lit. 'First Shankaracharya' was an 8th-century Indian Vedic scholar and teacher (*acharya*).

PART (III): ARE WE THERE YET?

The notion of a "one size fits all" approach to enlightenment, as represented by achieving signs or marks, oversimplifies the diverse and complex nature of human experiences. These static set of principles fails to capture the dynamic and ever-changing aspects of human existence that are derived from our individual intent.

The human body is a multifaceted entity, composed of numerous systems, organs, and processes, each with specific functions. The subjective nature of the body, as well as its existence within various social and cultural contexts, challenges the idea of a single, objective reality derived from a universal ontology.

Cultural factors can lead to different ideas of what constitutes an ethical or enlightened person. For example, some cultures view "mad" individuals as enlightened despite lacking conventional marks or signs of enlightenment. This diversity highlights the importance of personal perception and understanding of one's own spiritual path.

An alternative approach is the development of epistemic awareness[26], which involves understanding how individuals judge the plausibility of phenomena. Intentional learners, who prioritize mindsets built around skills of effective learning, can grow faster than their peers who blindly follow dogma. These learners treat every moment as a learning opportunity, recognizing the potential for growth in all experiences.

Embracing the significance of the body in localizing consciousness is essential for navigating this shape-shifting landscape. The embodiment of subjective experiences forms the foundation of meaning and understanding in our lives and is indispensable for calibrating our understanding of what consciousness truly is.

Schools that dismiss the body's significance fail to acknowledge that we are body consciousness foremost. Neglecting the body/mind/brain as a critical aspect of consciousness borders on intellectual dishonesty.

PART (IV): INSIDE-OUT PERSPECTIVE IS OUR ONLY REALITY

Rebecca Goldstein[27] **(Goldstein, 1983)** suggests that "consciousness is an intrinsic property of matter, and as we are composed of matter, *it is the singular property to which we have access*". Despite mathematical methods guiding our understanding of matter's relational properties, consciousness remains the one phenomenon we experience first-hand, while the intrinsic nature of matter stays enigmatic.

Some believe that consciousness persists beyond us as an objective reality, pointing to the disappearance of body consciousness during sleep or coma. This dualist view has been adopted by televangelists, preachers, and spiritual demagogues for centuries, who have attempted to define this elusive external consciousness. through this dualistic perspective.

---

26. Epistemic awareness refers to an individual's understanding of their own knowledge and beliefs, including their limitations, sources, and the processes through which they are formed or changed.

27. Rebecca Goldstein - Wikipedia; Goldstein, R. (1983). The Mind Body Problem. Penguin.

Such conjectures stem from the Outside-In approach, prevalent in mainstream religious thought, which downplays the subjective experience of the individual.

It should be obvious that each person possesses a spontaneously operating brain, creating unique experiences or qualia. This inner realm, more genuine than any shared reality, constitutes a singular experience of consciousness.

The Inside-Out approach, which acknowledges subjective experiences rather than averaging conjectures into dogma or ideology, provides a more valid path to understanding consciousness. Individuals create subjective experiences and derive meaning and purpose through the Inside-Out approach.

Since the late 20th century, experiments in neuroscience, quantum biology, and quantum mechanics have confirmed body consciousness as the first point of contact with our conscious experience. (*We discuss a few of these studies in subsequent chapters.*)

The allure of bumper sticker gurus and dream merchants who peddle ancient dogma and lofty goals that eclipse the individual's subjective reality is a temptation that many succumb to. After all, why think when it is easier to believe in what the group or the collective thinks to fit in??

This external dependence to achieve the "Alayavijnana", the Body of Consciousness,, the all-knowing field, is the Buddha's Stairway to Heaven. A prospect, that bears a striking resemblance to an all-encompassing cybernetic Metaverse wrapped around artificial intelligence that will deliver a TechnoUtopia where all of humanity's problems will be solved. (*We cover this in the following chapter*)

Chapter 5

Stairway to Heaven, the Metaverse Fantasy (Continuation of Verse 4, 5)

In our previous chapter, I introduced the intricate concept of "Alayavijnana," or the "Body of Consciousness,"

This enigmatic and abstract Alayavijnana has drawn comparisons with Quantum Physics, where, matter, and energy engage in a ceaseless dance of transformation, and by transmuting into each other dimensions of space and time are not fixed.[28]

This enthralling concept characterized by the constant unfolding and rejuvenation of the Alayavijnana has captured the interest of AI enthusiasts as well. These AI enthusiasts passionately avow that AI will ceaselessly learn and refine itself, augmenting its own capabilities. By embracing this self-improving AI, which operates at a velocity surpassing that of the entire human population, we aim to transcend our inherent limitations to arrive at TechnoUtopia.

In this chapter, I explore the seductive notion of AI as a comprehensive solution to humanity's problems, a system we now allege can outsmart our own intellectual capacities. We will grapple with the implications of such beliefs: Are we, in our pursuit of progress, at risk of sacrificing the essence of our humanity to the cold efficiency of mechanized output?

I became acutely aware of AI's cold, impersonal nature during my battle with COVID-19 from November 2021 to January 2022., As I lay unconscious, I was ironically awakened to the dehumanizing aspects of

---

28.   Capra, F. (1975). The Tao of Physics. Shambala

AI. Encased within a sterile ICU environment, and the drugs dulling my senses, I felt a disconnection between my body and mind.

The healthcare staff, resembling floating figures from a dystopian novel, moved robotically in their protective gear, deepened my sensory isolation. As I flickered between consciousness, I found myself unable to differentiate between objects and their context. I had lost my tactile sensations, which normally would be vital in comprehending my environment and *locus standi.* I felt like I was floating in a void, unable to connect with the physical world. My once vibrant body was a mere appendage to the life-supporting machines. My awareness blurred the line between human and machine; I struggled to comprehend my surroundings, amplifying the gulf between sensation and understanding.

This scenario mirrored the Metaverse's ambition to merge individuals through virtual reality, highlighting the rift it creates between our physical selves and real-world interactions.

This disorienting experience underscored the crucial role of our physical bodies in shaping our perception. The notion *"I am not this body, nor the mind"* was clearly misleading; indeed disregarding the body as the primary interpreter of the world was misguided and delusional.

During my recovery, I wondered how we ended up reducing human complexity to mechanical processes, a failing I attribute largely to our educational system.

Educational institutions have somehow made us believe that all activities in life are just mechanistic procedures; machines that can be managed by computational rules and algorithms. Machines that automate tasks, no matter how good they are at performing them, can't have consciousness, can't feel an inner subjective experience, and can't spontaneously express emotions. Simply put, they can't understand or express the full range of human experience.

Understanding that machines are built to calculate, and our minds are built to think and comprehend, it is therefore imperative to question why we're so captivated by our digital selves, our Avatars in the Metaverse.

Could this fascination hint at a far more dangerous possibility that we're beginning to accept a limited view of our humanity—one that can be reduced to computational algorithms alone?

The growth of AI is a fantastic technological development, and it will play a dominant role in humanity's future. However, we must first understand the extent and limits of AI in relation to our own spontaneous qualia and how it is holding back our creativity and authenticity. Unfortunately, we believe AI will not only do the thinking for us but outthink us and tell us what and how to behave, choose, and direct our lives. We treat the Avatar we have created as an independent intelligence and a Silicon Deity that will direct our lives in every way, reducing us to mere commodities of code that can be made obsolete!

The potential for the Metaverse to dehumanize embodied connections to the real world is enormous. For instance, the Metaverse's ability to fabricate an alternate "reality" or a simulated one other than the physical one can only be accessed by those in a position to afford and understand it. It is a technology designed by elites, and for elites and implicitly leaves behind much of humanity in its wake[29].

Professor Reid, of Hope's Department of Mathematics, Computer Science, and Engineering, argues for overall control as well as the gathering and protection of data.

Professor Reid says that *"People have been talking about how the rise of Artificial Intelligence (AI) will significantly change society and everything we do. And that's true. But the metaverse is at least as big, if not bigger, than the rise of AI."*

"Because if you think about the way it works, the metaverse's ultimate aim is not just virtual reality or augmented reality, it's mixed reality (MR). It's blending the digital and the real world together. Ultimately this blend may be so good, and so pervasive, that the virtual and the real become indistinguishable. "And the market for that is gigantic. Whoever controls it, will basically have control over your entire reality."

Why are we so obsessed with the idea that everything can be reduced to computational algorithms? Why are we worshipping the feet of AI and thinking it's going to solve all our problems? Are we really just machines? Can a computer dream? No, but we can. And we have this whole inner world that's full of feelings and experiences that machines just can't replicate.

We are being led by the richest people on the planet who have decided that humanity has reached its limitations and needs to be augmented by machines. Like my body tethered to machines in the ICU that communicated my vital signs to my distant caregivers, many people

---

29.   Opinion | Why We Should Reject Mark Zuckerberg's Dehumanizing Vision of a "Metaverse" | Common Dreams

believe a **Mind-Machine Interface**, like **Neuralink**[30], is sufficient to replace human connections.

Their vision is of Human Plus, not Humanity Plus.

In the corporate world, our obsession with measuring everything has led CEOs to focus solely on tangible and measurable outcomes, missing out on the creativity and authenticity of their own employees. People are being treated like cogs in a machine, and that's a terrible retardation of our evolutionary potential. The risks posed by the Metaverse centre on overall control as well as the gathering and protection of data[31.]

Many are beginning to argue that it poses 'terrifying dangers' and that we need to figure out how to police it now before it's too late.

If we must put the genie back in the bottle it is imperative to shift our focus from mechanical paradigms to creative production, but that's not going to be easy. We need to embrace our transpersonal encounters with each other and start realizing that our consciousness and creativity can only be understood from an inside-out approach.

To achieve a genuine future of Humanity 3.0 and to end Humanity 2.0, we may need to reconsider the principles of creation within the Hermetic tradition, or the Imaginal world described by the great neo-Platonian Sufi, Surhawardy[32]. These templates can be useful to create a transhumanistic future, not just a human-plus future augmented by the mechanistic Metaverse that limits our humanness.

---

30.   Home - Neuralink

31.   The metaverse poses 'terrifying dangers,' academic warns (techxplore.com)

32.   Suhrawardi the Sufi was a Persian philosopher and mystic who lived in the 12th century. He is best known as the founder of the Illuminationist school of philosophy, which is based on the idea that knowledge is gained through illumination, or direct experience of the divine. (Marcotte, 2023); Marcotte, R. (2023). Suhrawardi. {The {Stanford} Encyclopedia of Philosophy}.

By combining our intuition with our intellect, we can tap into the vast potential of our consciousness and create a future that goes beyond our current limitations. We need to stop treating ourselves and each other as machines and instead embrace the richness of our subjective experiences.

The growth of AI is an exciting development, but we must not lose sight of our humanness in the process. We need a paradigm shift, both individually and within influential entities like corporations and governments. Rather than fixating solely on quantifiable outcomes, we must also prioritize creativity, authenticity, and our tangible connection to the physical world.

Chapter 6

(Verse 6, 7) – Drinking the Bath Water of the New Intelligentsia.

VERSE 6: RARE IS TRUE FAITH

Subhuti said to Buddha: World-honoured One, will there always be men who will truly believe after coming to hear these teachings? Buddha answered: Subhuti, do not utter such words! At the end of the last five hundred-year period following the passing of the Tathagata, there will be self controlled men, rooted in merit, coming to hear these teachings, who will be inspired with belief. But you should realize that such men have not strengthened their root of merit under just one Buddha, or two Buddhas, or three, or four, or five Buddhas, but under countless Buddhas; and their merit is of every kind. Such men, coming to hear these teachings, will have an immediate uprising of pure faith, Subhuti; and the Tathagata will recognize them. Yes, He will clearly perceive all these of pure heart, and the magnitude of their moral excellences. Wherefore? It is because such men will not fall back to cherishing the idea of an ego-entity, a personality, a being, or a separated individuality. They will neither fall back to cherishing the idea of things as having intrinsic qualities, nor even of things as devoid of intrinsic qualities. Wherefore? Because if such men allowed their minds to grasp and hold on to anything they would be cherishing the idea of an ego-entity, a personality, a being, or a separated individuality; and if they grasped and held on to the notion of things as having intrinsic qualities they would be cherishing the idea of an ego-entity, a personality, a being, or a separated individuality. Likewise, if they grasped and held on to the notion of things as devoid of intrinsic qualities they would be cherishing the idea of an ego-entity, a personality, a being, or a separated individuality. So you should not be attached to things as being possessed of, or devoid of, intrinsic qualities. This is the reason why the Tathagata always teaches this saying: My teaching of the Good Law is to be likened unto a raft. [Does a man who has safely crossed a flood upon a raft continue his journey carrying that raft upon his head?] The Buddha-teaching must be relinquished; how much more so mis-teaching

The authors of the Diamond Sutra possess a mastery of marketing techniques, boldly showcasing their brilliance in harnessing literary devices such as the Diamond Sutra as potent weapons of propaganda. Through their edict to simply recite the text for *Moksha*, they forge an unshakeable devotion to the Diamond Sutra, leaving no room for doubt or wavering loyalty. However, this verse reveals their underlying doubt, as they contemplate whether their "copy" would endure the relentless test of time.

Not unlike the authors of the Diamond Sutra, our present-day elites in the contemporary landscape have adeptly capitalized on our inherent inclination to embrace seemingly intelligent utilities like AI, and our innate susceptibility to defer to external authorities, especially propaganda. Exploiting these deeply ingrained predispositions, they deftly wield social media as covert instruments of subtle coercion, deftly manipulating and exerting control over our perceptions. Their aim is to ensure the seamless acceptance of their concealed agenda.

This chapter discusses the intricate mechanisms of this subliminal manipulation orchestrated by the intellectual elite, as they skillfully bind our biases and mold our thoughts. It seeks to evoke introspection, urging us to critically examine the extent of our autonomy as independent thinkers. I hope it would prompt the reader to contemplate whether the notion of free will endures amid the seductive allure of TechnoUtopia and the Metaverse.

Circling back to this Verse, a significant point of interest is the portrayal of Buddha as offering a "prediction" concerning the reception of this documented dialogue, nearly five centuries after his demise. These so-called 'prophetic' utterances indicate that Buddha, as a character, is well aware of the discourse's longevity as a publication in the future.

Subhuti's scepticism in his question, *"Will there be beings who will truly believe after hearing these teachings?"* is met with a retort from Buddha: *"Subhuti, do not utter such words!"* This robust reproach not only reassures Subhuti and future disciples but also confirms a strong intent at evangelizing, where doubt is unwelcome, aiming to unify its followers to extend the Sangha.

This specific portion of the Diamond Sutra seems to extend the edicts from the preceding verses, giving it the appearance of an appendage to earlier chapters 4 and 5. Both those verses, 4 and 5, underscore the identification of signs and marks and stress the significance of ethical conduct as a pathway to Nirvana. It reinforces the requirement of an unwavering devotion to the text which implies implicit acceptance of the Sutras would lead a devotee to *Moksha*, themes that recur throughout the Diamond Sutra.

Examinations of the Diamond Sutra as a literary device are infrequent, and critiques of it as a carefully designed tool for proselytization, aimed at swaying a broad audience, are even rarer. Nevertheless, for those genuinely interested in understanding early Buddhism, its evolution, and its fragmentation into various doctrines and schools—including "Western" Buddhism—it is worthwhile to scrutinize this section for its evangelizing *modus operandi.*

To begin exploring the mass appeal of the Sutra down the ages, it is necessary to comprehend the significance of this heavily pregnant statement in the verse *"500 years after the passing of the Tathagatha,"*.

Examining this from a historical standpoint, the claim that the Dharma would only endure for 500 years draws attention to the theological tension that existed between the early Mahayana and Nikaya schools during the establishment of the Pali Canon. The background of this friction becomes necessary if we have to decipher why the author of the Diamond Sutra is introducing such a line.

Essentially, the Nikaya school took the Buddha's statement about The Dharma's limited lifespan literally, interpreting it as an indication that his teachings would become corrupted 500 years after his death. In contrast. the Mahayana school believed that the Abhidharma corpus[33] had made the Buddha's teachings stagnant and sought to reinterpret and reinvigorate them.

The fundamental divergence in perspective between these schools led to debates and disagreements, particularly regarding the interpretation of Buddhist scriptures and the nature of ultimate reality. This contrasted with the Nikaya schools, which focused on the concept of dependent origination[34] and posited that all phenomena arise dependent on other factors and conditions.

The main thrust of the Madhyamika school, founded by Nagarjuna, emphasized the concept of emptiness (Shunyata) and asserted that all phenomena lack inherent existence and were interdependent.

Such tensions between the old and the new, the static and the regenerative, the reverent and the irreverent, are often overlooked by religious Buddhist schools when interpreting the expansion of Buddhism. To fully appreciate the ideas they present, it is crucial to accept that **all**

---

33.   Abhidharma - Wikipedia

34.   Dependent origination, also known as Paticca-samuppada in the Nikaya school
       of Buddhism, is the concept that everything arises in dependence upon multiple
       causes and conditions

breakthroughs are born out of healthy scepticism and critical thought-even heresy.

The renaissance that Nagarjuna introduced began 600 years earlier in Greece with the Milesians marking a significant shift of Humanity's from traditional narratives of gods and demons towards seeking answers through first-hand experience and critical thought.

Before the Milesians, the Greeks and many other cultures ascribed reality to stories of anthropomorphic gods and goddesses, attributing natural phenomena to their actions. Their beliefs were perceived as self-evident and infallible. However, **Thales** and **Anaximander** sought answers through observation and reason, initiating a new era of critical thinking that questioned the dogmas and assumptions of the past.

This innovative approach to acquiring knowledge of direct experience deviated from the traditional dependence on dogma, introducing the suspension of judgment and certainty. The Milesians' methodology laid the groundwork for subsequent Greek and Roman philosophers and the advent of Pyrrhonism (later evolved into Vedanta) in the subcontinent[35.] It signalled the genesis of scientific thought and the foundations of scepticism.

The revolution in thinking and the challenge of external and untested sources, such as myths of gods and goddesses, gave rise to the Western world's critical paradigm for advancing understanding and exploring reality. The approach extended beyond scientific inquiry, integrating scepticism into our thinking to expand our consciousness and investigate the unknown. These early days of epistemic reasoning[36] laid the foundation for future intellectual growth.

Even in modern times, many societies, and religious groups, like the Nikaya, steadfastly hold onto sacred dogmas, thereby limiting their capacity for inquiry and exploration. To revisit the main thrust of my

---

35. Most of this intermingling were facilitated first by the conquest of Alexander and then subsequently Greek-Indo kings. Greco-Buddhism (mcgill.ca)

36. Epistemology | Definition, History, Types, Examples, Philosophers, & Facts | Britannica

argument, a significant portion of humanity is conditioned to adhere to these dogmas, predisposing us to venerate any external authority perceived as more credible. This attitude is reflected in our embrace of a cybernetic world powered by AI, often ignoring our own intuition.

I feel it is vital to discern between our first-hand experiences and the inferences or conjectures drawn from texts or external authorities. If we can't extract purpose and meaning from the texts we read, or interpret reality based on our personal perspectives, we are not reading the sutras, but rather the sutras reading us. Similarly, without independent thinking, it's not us controlling Artificial Intelligence, but AI that's manipulating us. It is not Mind over matter, but matter over mind.

Direct perception out of our inner theatre encourages us to view reality from our individual perspectives, rather than accepting conjectured interpretations from preachers. It's essential that we insist our preachers and gurus differentiate between the inferred realities they speculate on and the ones we derive from our direct experiences and inner truth.

As the **Kalama Sutra**[37] emphasizes, it is crucial to examine teachings through direct experience from our epistemic awareness only. Teachings should inspire rather than dogmatically dictate absolute truth. The seeds of the Milesian revolution in thinking have endowed the Western Hemisphere with a critical paradigm for advancing our understanding of the world and exploring reality. It is vital to question our ideas of the known if they do not withstand observational scrutiny. Our evolving comprehension of consciousness thrives on creatively dismantling the known, so we can explore and expand into the unknown.

---

37. "now look you all kalamas, do not be led by reports, or tradition, or hearsay. Be not be led but the authority of religious texts, nor by mere logic or inference, nor by considering appearances, nor by the delight in speculated opinions, nor by seeming possibilities not by the idea: 'this is our teacher' or 'This is our Teaching'. But O Kalamas, when you know for yourself that certain things are unwholesome (akusala), and wrong and bad then give them up and then you know for yourself that certain things are wholesome (kusala) and good then accept them and follow them.

And yet, in the contemporary world, the modern mind still grapples with those fetters imposed by those in power through the dogma of ideology.

Today, we see this power wielded by the ultra-wealthy and influential political elites, who urge us toward their vision of a TechnoUtopia. The propaganda and subtle threat used by these elites is that non-adoption and non-compliance with these AI technologies will leave those behind in the wake of a society that is adopting AI under the canopy of uniformity and development.

Not unlike the not-so-subtle message of this Verse in the Diamond Sutra: *"in compliance to accepting the sanctity of the Sutra, one may find the path to Moksha".*

This new intelligentsia contends that human free will is overrated and that our diversity of opinions poses a threat to order. Their idea of progress involves designing AI systems, such as OpenAI, Metaverse, and Baidu, to monitor and regulate every facet of daily life, with the assurance of fostering harmony and happiness among the masses. Accustomed to AI's guidance, we have grown complacent, apathetic, and devoid of initiative.

This is the bathwater of the new intelligentsia that we now lap up.

In a desperate bid to reclaim their autonomy, individuals indulge in peculiar pastimes such as synchronized laugh-a-thons, extreme thumb wrestling, competitions, competitive nose-picking, attacking random folk and filming it on TikTok to get the maximum views, and self-produced pornographic videos. All this trivia is celebrated and encouraged by rich idiots breeding more idiots through the idiot box. This banality is considered today's aspirational goal. Though these pursuits may appear trivial, they represent people's yearning to assert their independence, by asserting their relevance through the thrill of making their own choices, however banal or clichéd they may be.

Further, it should be obvious this centralization of power among those who control AI and big data poses a threat to privacy, diversity, and competition. Nationalistic governments prioritize uniformity over diversity, as well as granting unchecked control to their favoured oligarchy. The new elite's sway over AI development may give rise to ethical transgressions, with their interests superseding those of the majority.

As AI permeates every aspect of existence and hypnotizing us into a semblance of order and harmony, individuals find themselves ensnared within a gilded cage of predictability.

Even though many won't admit it, people long for a time when they were free to make mistakes, learn and grow from those experiences. The new intelligentsia's vision of a harmonious society with decisions made by Artificial Intelligence has paved the path for a life devoid of growth and fulfillment, leaving entire communities bereft of creativity and spontaneity.

I reiterate: Our predisposition to be subjugated by the new intelligentsia can be traced back to indoctrination by religious and political elite, which has diminished the critical thinking faculties of entire communities.

Unfortunately, achieving autonomy through the cultivation of independent thought presents a formidable threat to this intelligentsia and the influential elite. To countervail this threat of independent thought and scepticism, society is subjected to a relentless deluge of propaganda, convincing us to accept and embrace the narrative proffered by those in authority. This narrative asserts that the more we depend on AI technology, the happier we shall become. Analogous to the prisoners in Plato's allegorical cave, we are permitted only to see the shadows, limiting our exposure to anything beyond the cave. Or, like the wooden axe persuading a tree of its inevitable fate to be chopped, simply because both are made of wood, society continues to accept and believe in the narrative imposed by those in power.

Thus, we are imprisoned within this gilded cage of AI, as we have been led to believe that measurements and definitions are the sum of the world, which restricts our ability to experience reality beyond its confines.

In the face of our modern society's preoccupation with the algorithms and codes that seem to dictate every aspect of our lives, the task of establishing true autonomy through independent thought can be a daunting one, for even the most intellectually astute among us. Indeed, those who express any degree of scepticism towards this blind adoration of technology are often met with fierce resistance in their professional and social spheres alike.

As the physicist **Carlo Rovelli** so eloquently reminds us, there is a solution to this conundrum - one that lies in the power of our own individual minds. By cultivating a robust and independent thought process, we can begin to break free from the shackles of conformity and carve out a unique path for ourselves in this ever-evolving world. He says:

"By continuously refining our worldview, we can uncover hidden aspects of reality that elude common perception. The capacity for discovering novelty lies in embracing a distinctive style of thinking. In this approach, disciples are free to build upon their master's ideas, unafraid to critique or discard what can be improved. This presents a balanced middle ground between strict adherence to an ideology and wholesale dismissal of ideas. Such a mindset is crucial for advancing philosophical and scientific thought. From this point forward, knowledge expands at an unprecedented rate, fuelled by past insights as well as by the potential for critical evaluation and enhancement of our understanding."

Scepticism is the first step that serves as our vessel for transcending the limitations imposed by this new intelligentsia. We don't need to be swayed by the overwhelming pressures of conformity, instead, we can listen to the call of our own individual spirits, and in doing so, establish a sense of true autonomy that is both liberating and empowering. For it is only through independent thought that we can truly unlock the limitless potential that lies within each one of us.

As this verse states, *"Does a man who has safely crossed a flood upon a raft continue his journey carrying that raft upon his head? The Buddha-teaching must be relinquished; how much more so mis-teaching?"*

Perhaps the true message of this verse is: The most profound education resides in the process of unlearning. It involves the graceful abandonment of the raft of misguided doctrines - dogmas that neither serve a purpose nor aid in our evolutionary journey.

VERSE 7: GREAT ONES, PERFECT BEYOND LEARNING, UTTER NO WORDS OF TEACHING

Subhuti, what do you think? Has the Tathagata attained the Consummation of Incomparable Enlightenment? Has the Tathagata a teaching to enunciate? Subhuti answered: As I understand Buddha's meaning there is no formulation of truth called Consummation of Incomparable Enlightenment.

Moreover, the Tathagata has no formulated teaching to enunciate. Wherefore? Because the Tathagata has said that truth is uncontainable and inexpressible. It neither is nor is it not. Thus it is that this unformulated Principle is the foundation of the different systems of all the sages.

This verse stands out for its straightforwardness and brevity. While some interpret it as a contradiction to the earlier verse that stresses the importance of reverence for the text, I believe it stands out due to its unique writing style and assertiveness. Given the Diamond Sutra's and other early Buddhist texts' aim to proselytize, Verse 6 was not simply crafted for theatrical impact. Verse 7 is reminiscent of the authorship seen in the Diamond Sutra's first verse which suggests no effort is required; in this instance, the author implies that freedom is a pathless journey. Such contrasting penmanship also bolsters my belief that the text was crafted by a consortium of writers, each injecting their unique perspectives.

The core message of this verse is that studying the texts isn't merely for scholarship but directs one to self-discovery. If one realizes this truth, all texts should be forsaken in favour of introspection.

The phrase *"Because the Tathagata has said that truth is uncontainable and inexpressible"* is pregnant with implications and a tacit admission that consciousness cannot be defined. For a more comprehensive discussion on this line, and similar verses that allude to the deficiency of language, the reader can jump to Chapter 10: *"Words mean nothing, because Words turn back…."*

Chapter 7

Where are the 10,000 Buddhas?"
(Verse 8)

VERSE 8: THE FRUITS OF MERITORIOUS ACTION

Subhuti, what do you think? If anyone filled three thousand galaxies of worlds with the seven treasures and gave all away in gifts of alms, would he gain great merit? Subhuti said: Great indeed, World- honoured One! Wherefore? Because merit partakes of the character of no-merit, the Tathagata characterized the merit as great.

Then Buddha said: On the other hand, if anyone received and retained even only four lines of this Discourse and taught and explained them to others, his merit would be the greater.

Wherefore? Because, Subhuti, from this Discourse issue forth all the Buddhas and the Consummation of Incomparable Enlightenment teachings of all the Buddhas.

Subhuti, what is called "the Religion given by Buddha" is not, in fact Buddha Religion

This verse tightens Buddhism's proselytization-through-scripture strategy. It doesn't merely advocate for the expansion of the faith—it presents a compelling proposition: by reciting a mere four lines from the Diamond Sutra, one is seemingly offered an expedited path towards spiritual enlightenment, akin to discovering a shortcut to reach Nirvana.

This intriguing assurance may have played a significant role in the rapid expansion of Buddhism throughout Asia. For many seekers, the allure of a shortcut to spiritual attainment would have been compelling. The prospect of bypassing years of arduous practice and discipline in favour of a more direct route to transcendental consciousness would have had considerable appeal.

This verse, with its potent claim, would have captured the imaginations of those who encountered it, sparking curiosity, and potentially inspiring them to delve deeper into Buddhist teachings. As a result, the message of Buddhism could spread more rapidly, transcending geographical and cultural boundaries, and gaining momentum as it reached new audiences. It reminds us that even in the context of ancient wisdom traditions, the promise of a shortcut to enlightenment may have been a driving force behind the expansion of a faith that has endured for millennia.

This unique verse demonstrates the power of ideas and the influence that a single concept can have on the course of a religious movement. Nudge theorists might see this as a fine example of copywriting to modify consumer behaviour.

As I pointed out earlier, the simplicity of Buddhist practices, grounded in common-sense ethics instead of long drawn-out rituals, enticed spiritual seekers with the promise of not only transcendence in their current life but also the prospect of attaining higher states of Arahat and Bodhisattva. Buddhism's early days emphasized the Avadana theology, which underscored the importance of ethical practices and introspection throughout numerous lifetimes. This bonded aspirants to an ethical journey spanning lifetimes which was a reward in and of itself, not solely the destination of Nirvana. If the destination was elusive, then selling the idea that the journey was a reward in itself, would bind those to the path!

As time progressed, esoteric practices like Tantra and meditation techniques emerged alongside these ethical practices. The **Ajivikas**[38]— an organized ascetic sect predating the birth of Buddha and Mahavira— gained popularity among those living on the fringes of Vedic society. Their 'mind' gymnastics offered individuals direct subjective experiences, offering them glimpses of their inner higher dimensions and liberating them from the dominance of any external priestly authority.

This environment and tradition that denied lower social strata access to the Vedas[39] created a ripe opportunity for an alternative ideology like Buddhism that could be easily accessed and disseminated to the common people and lower castes.

During this era, emerging literary works, including the Diamond Sutra, the *Lotus Sutra*, and the *Vimalakirti Sutra*, became familiar to large sections of societies. Ironically, the Mahayana School, which employed scepticism to counter the Nikaya School's blind worship of texts, found itself competing with other theological traditions as well. The Mahayana School derided the Nikaya, dubbing them a cult of sutra worshippers. However, the exhortation in this verse that reciting just four lines of the Diamond Sutra would grant the disciple "the rarest and the most exalted of Dharmas" contradicts their own core teaching! This final line holds great significance for readers who wish to understand how Buddhism spread so rapidly.

The first part of the Diamond Sutra is well-organized, but it begins to unravel and become disconnected from this verse onward. The Sutra subsequently shifts to a predominantly recursive emphasis on practicing ethics to access the Buddha's "Stairway to Heaven."

✳✳✳

The rise of spiritual literature was catapulted by the invention of printing after the Chinese developed printing around 250 BCE and the Indians

---

38.   Ajivikas - Their History and Philosophy (hinduwebsite.com)

39.   Vedas - Wikipedia

adopted it six centuries later. The ability to disseminate a message through print media was exciting for the earliest Buddhist missionaries. The copying of scripture was listed as the first of ten essential religious practices by 4th-century master Asanga. With that command to worship, the earliest Mahayana texts were being copied and proliferated at an industrial scale. The adoption of Buddhism in the Far East could be compared to the success of viral social media marketing today.

The Diamond Sutra is an example of spiritual literature that promotes the idea that reading the text as a deified object can propel the reader into a position of the most exalted. – Because it implies the Buddha resides in the text and reading just four lines is sufficient to obtain the grace of the Buddha.

The error in such a proposition that reading sacred text alone could alter one's consciousness arose from the notion that language and thought were built on a system of logical propositions, with a perfect one-to-one correspondence between the structure of the proposition and the structure of the world or reality. This view is often referred to as the "picture theory" of language, where meaningful propositions accurately reflects states of consciousness within ourselves. Even today, such blind acceptance of text adheres to the belief that philosophical propositions could convey meaningful information about the world and reality[40]

Language is not a rigid, logical system but rather a flexible, social practice that is deeply rooted in the shared activities and customs of human life. Language and thought are not simply reducible to a set of logical propositions and static labels and definitions that mirror the world, but are instead embedded in the rich tapestry of human social practices and how each of us ascribes different meanings and intent to our communication (Biletzki, 2021).

On its own, the text can do nothing, and even if it could enlighten everyone, none of us would be enlightened the same way. Like a painting that evokes a subjective experience, the text may provide insight based on our individual intent that cannot be replicated or described.

---

40.   Biletzki, 2021.

Both the Sutras and AI codes composed by humans are artifacts within the Universal Mind. Both can impinge on our individual consciousness, as we humans are also an artifact within the Universal Mind!

Similarly, the view that objects or artifacts, such as four lines of a verse, are independent sources to originate a higher consciousness is like our modern humanity's acceptance that artificial intelligence and neural networks would eventually deliver Artificial Consciousness in place of our own creativity.

The canon of today is the computer language we call code. (More of this later.)

Elon Musk, the world's favourite technocrat, has promoted a new brain chip from his company "Neuralink," Musk stated the chips "hold promise for the restoration of sensory and motor function and the treatment of neurological disorders." The Brain-Machine Interface[41], or BMI, that implants chips onto the brain, could "solve a lot of brain/spine injuries.[42.]

This is an excellent example of how technology should be used to address human challenges. But at the same time, Elon goes on to say he could pipe music directly onto the brain! Have we considered the implications of an external entity leveraging artificial intelligence to direct or influence our thinking process? Have we considered the impact when it comes to others' agendas or decisions that employ AI to delineate what we should think or disregard? This Frankenstein scenario is not new when we look at past political landscapes where autocratic regimes despots and religious demagogues have demonstrated how our cognitive biases can be influenced. It is vital to consider the implications of a 'thought curator', be it AI or otherwise, that could infringe on our autonomy of thought and decision-making. Our ability to think freely,

---

41. A **brain–machine interface (BMI)** or **smartbrain**, is a direct communication pathway between the brain's electrical activity and an external device, most commonly a computer or robotic limb

42. Marc P. Powell, 2023

form opinions, and make choices is a fundamental human right. Any AI system or agenda that may impinge on this freedom ought to be critically examined.

As parents, many of us are exasperated when our children are glued to smartphones. Today's Social Media or what is now referred to as the Surveillance Economy, which keeps them glued to their screens feeding them a virtual world of banality. What if Neuralink doesn't restrict itself to just paralyzed people and this use of this Body Mind Interface (BMI) device is used on able-bodied people as well? Musk's vision is to see a future where people can control smart devices without having to interact with them physically. Neuralink's goal is to build an interface that enables someone's brain to control a smartphone or computer and to make this process routine as Lasik surgery.

There is a delicate balance between embracing the benefits of technology and becoming passive recipients of external influences. It is imperative we become active participants in shaping our own lives and preserving our individuality and freedom of thought.

Furthermore, a crucial question to consider is whether a technology-driven utopia can truly address all social ills, historical injustices, and traumas. This question is vital for humanity's future. Despite numerous valuable technological advancements, AI systems cannot generate motivation or empathy with other computers to solve humanity's problems. Only humans, and some higher mammals, display empathy through social interactions.

Emotions and feelings are necessary to begin understanding another's suffering. It doesn't begin with computers; it emerges and ends within us. Only after we define a problem can we choose to utilize AI's numerical and brute-force problem-solving abilities.

Today, our public discourse is at an all-time low. The internet and social media, with their viral capabilities, are mostly responsible. A single malicious comment online can trigger a wave of violent reactions, engulfing entire communities and societies. Despite evidence to the contrary, someone can claim the election was stolen, inciting their followers to storm the seats of power. Why is it that we are so ready to follow a mob without verifying facts or fostering scepticism, and how does this human tendency to follow the herd blindly get exploited by those in power?

History is filled with wars resulting from bruised egos and misunderstandings, leading to atrocities, cultural displacement, normalization of slavery, and human-caused famines. The algorithms of platforms like Twitter and Facebook, which intentionally pit us against one another, make us question whether nations are looking toward a global Armageddon.

I've observed hostility between people from STEM and humanities backgrounds, who dismiss the qualitative aspects of human cognition as trivial and incorrectly quantified attributes. The STEM evangelist's logic is that quantitative thinking is considered more capable of producing meaning in life.

However, the scientific mind is not the only way to achieve coherence in an incoherent universe. Yet, it takes centre stage in our educational systems and corporate boardrooms. The dominant areas of human creativity, derived from interactions with society, are side-lined by quantitative fields.

There's a parallel to be drawn with the "**Rich Dad, Poor Dad**[43] analogy, as we now grapple with the "*Tech Dad, Non-Tech Dad*" dichotomy. Many parents have wholly embraced the notion that specializing in coding and focusing on STEM subjects alone assures lifelong employment—a pipe dream that has turned into a nightmare.

Our children, nudged into the labyrinth of coding and technology, often find themselves with no critical life skills when the IT industry cannot assimilate a workforce that has been reduced to commoditized individuals by our educational bias and infatuation with STEM subjects.

Indeed, the advent of AI tools has starkly highlighted the extent of our self-commodification. As we transition to an era where automated

---

43.   (Kiyosaki, 2001)"

coding becomes the norm, it brings into sharp relief our necessity for resilience, adaptability, and an array of competencies beyond mere technical expertise.

I submit, in the advent of this technologically complex era, the skills of coding, while important, should not be mistaken as the only requisite skill to thrive. Talent scouts now recognize the cross-pollination of knowledge is increasingly vital for fresh and unique perspectives in the workplace. Today's tech industry thirsts for professionals who, like Renaissance men and women, can intertwine insights from varied fields such as ethics, business, humanities, and design, and interlace them with their technical prowess.

Margaret Mead, the renowned anthropologist, emphasizes the crucial role of empathy and caring in our world and the skills required in interactions with society when she said, *"Never believe that a few caring people can't change the world. For, indeed, that's all who ever have."*

This quote on empathy attributed to Margaret Mead followed the discovery of an ancient thigh bone that showed signs of having been broken and later healed. In the animal kingdom, a broken femur meant abandonment and certain death, but in the emerging human civilization, the healed bone indicated someone had cared for and nurtured the injured person. This is indicative of a mature civilization, according to Mead. Even if she did not actually say this, I think the message is vital to understand that our future lies in an empathic response to each other and the cross-functional skills we need to impart to the next generation.

If individuals neglect the cultivation of empathy and fail to embrace humanity's inherent imperfections—factors that inspire us to seek change—then AI and technology become devoid of the necessary human touch needed to drive new inventions and innovations.

Job loss extends beyond the Darwinian concept of survival of the fittest; it carries a deeper and more unsettling implication. When corporations swap human labour for AI, it portrays people as expendable entities, analogous to disposable lines of code or exhausted cogs in vast industrial machinery. What compounds this tragedy is that this vision is propagated by some of the most intellectually endowed individuals on the planet—PhDs and CXOs—who fail to recognize that reducing human capabilities to mere machine output fundamentally strips us of our humanity.

Our steadfast belief in canon and code, often viewed as the ultimate solutions for spiritual enlightenment and economic advancement, tends to overshadow the significance of fostering human connections. This imbalance threatens to devalue the richness and depth of human relationships and personal growth, potentially compromising our collective humanity in the pursuit of progress.

Years ago, this reliance on external authority and 'sacred' texts came sharply into focus for me during the commemoration of the Dalai Lama's escape from Tibet, held in Dharamshala, India. The gathering was a riot of languages, a babel of voices from every corner of the globe. Strangers, their faces luminous with the comfort of a common connection, greeted one another as if they were old friends, transcending the barriers of the unfamiliar.

At the heart of the event, the Dalai Lama held court before an ocean of devotees, who were draped in robes of ochre and burgundy. As my eyes scanned the crowd, noting the preponderance of Westerners, I couldn't help but observe their choice of attire. The *Civara*, a garment prescribed for monks in the Pali canon, was once a simple piece of clothing millennia ago. Yet, the way it adorned these aspirants today seemed like a cosmetic extravagance. What was the need to conceal their natural state, the natural expression of the Tathagatha of their humanity beneath the trappings of religious attire? Perhaps they believed just like this Verse, that, by reading four lines of the Diamond Sutra they would be transported to enlightenment, likewise, simply wearing the *Civara* would transfigure them into an enlightened state.

As the Dalai Lama settled onto his cushioned seat, the drone of voices dwindled to silence. The audience, poised for an enlightening discourse on some esoteric Buddhist tenet, shifted their butts on their seats and cushions and waited in anticipation.

But the Dalai Lama surprised us all. "How many of you are Buddhas?" he inquired, suddenly. "Surely, after so many years, the world should have at least 10,000 Buddhas, I think." Turning to a lady in the crowd and putting her in a spot, he pressed her for an answer, "Are you a Buddha? And you?" he asked another, his canned laughter dissipating the tension and the audience chuckled nervously in response.

"No?" he persisted, "Perhaps we can find ten Buddhas here today? Not even that? Surely, at least one!" His mirth became contagious, and the crowd laughed along, either blind to the gravity of his question or simply choosing to laugh away the uncomfortable insight.

The Dalai Lama's query was not mere rhetoric; it bore significant weight. After two and a half millennia of theological debate, years of rigorous ethical practice like 'Dana', and recitations of Sutras spanning days, as this verse directs, we should have seen the rise of at least 10,000 Buddhas!

In the context of our exploration of AI and consciousness, this incident may help us to better understand how our preoccupation with mechanistic solutions, such as rites and rituals, or scripts, whether spiritual or computational, can be a distraction from the richness and depth that can be found in human relationships and lived experience.

These prescribed wisdoms may provide structure and guidance, but they are no substitute for the personal development that can only come from genuine connection with others and the world around us.

If you've spent time on ClubHouse or similar platforms, you've probably noticed countless speakers who parrot the teachings of their mentors or holy texts as undeniable truths. This isn't just an online trend; it's a widespread practice among various religious leaders who assert their views on reality we should adopt. However, you'd likely agree that true meaning arises not from echoing others or engaging in abstract speculation, but from your personal interaction with the world.

Thought-provoking as they may be, philosophical and metaphysical musings often veer into abstraction, straying from the immediate, concrete experiences and the meaning we personally assign to them. A major flaw in this philosophical chatter is the omission of context from the life of the individual, which can lead to distortions of reality.

This disregard for context, particularly prevalent in today's online media, overlooks each listener's individual journey to understand their unique reality, can prove quite damaging to entire populations.

Having studied the Sutras and practiced the Eightfold Path and Four Noble Truths for many years, I must respectfully inquire: Are you a Buddha? If not, what would it take?

Chapter 8

"The Un-Being of You" (Verses 9, 10)

VERSE 9 : REAL DESIGNATION IS UNDESIGNATE

Subhuti, what do you think? Does a disciple who has entered the Stream of the Holy Life say within himself: I obtain the fruit of a Stream-entrant? Subhuti said: No, World-honoured One. Wherefore? Because "Stream entrant" is merely a name. There is no stream-entering. The disciple who pays no regard to form, sound, odour, taste, touch, or any quality, is called a Stream-entrant. Subhuti, what do you think? Does an adept who is subject to only one more rebirth say within himself: I obtain the fruit of a Once-to-be-reborn? Subhuti said: No, World-honoured One. Wherefore? Because "Once-to-be-reborn" is merely a name. There is no passing away nor coming into existence. [The adept who realizes] this is called "Once-to-be-reborn." Subhuti, what do you think? Does a venerable one who will never more be reborn as a mortal say within himself: I obtain the fruit of a Non-returner? Subhuti said: No, World-honoured One. Wherefore? Because "Non-returner" is merely a name. There is no non-returning; hence the designation "Nonreturner." Subhuti, what do you think? Does a holy one say within himself: I have obtained Perfective Enlightenment? Subhuti said: No, World-honoured One. Wherefore? Because there is no such condition as that called "Perfective Enlightenment." World-honoured one, if a holy one of Perfective Enlightenment said to himself "such am I," he would necessarily partake of the idea of an ego-entity, a personality, a being, or a separated individuality. World honoured One, when the Buddha declares that I excel amongst holy men in the Yoga of perfect quiescence, in dwelling in seclusion, and in freedom from passions, I do not say within myself: I am a holy one of Perfective Enlightenment, free from passions. World-honoured One, if I said within myself: Such am I; you would not declare: Subhuti finds happiness abiding in peace, in seclusion in the midst of the forest. This is because Subhuti abides nowhere: therefore he is called, "Subhuti, Joyful Abider-in-Peace, Dweller-in Seclusion-in-the-Forest."

This segment might be considered the linchpin of the entire commentary, and hopefully bring more clarity and depth to the preceding chapters.

My critique of these two verses isn't targeted at their explicit content, but rather, it addresses their notable silence on a crucial aspect – and that is, the primary role of our cognitive apparatus to grasp Consciousness via direct experience. This omission by the Sutra seems to undervalue our innate human ability to comprehend and connect with Consciousness first-hand.

Verse 9 introduces four spiritual personages or bodies in Nikaya Buddhism that aspirants should strive to attain through the practices of ethics as well as the edict below, like waypoints along the transcendent path[44].

To reach these stages, the verse states, "Because while Strottapanna means 'entering the stream,' there is no entering here. *A true Strottapanna is one who does not enter sound, odour, flavor, touch, or any thought that arises.*" Verse 10 reverberates this sentiment: "So, Subhuti, all Bodhisattvas, lesser and great, should develop a pure, lucid mind, *not*

---

44.   These stages of accomplishment or personages include the **Stream-entrant (Strottapanna), the Adept (Sakridagamin), the Venerable One (Anagamin), and the Holy One (Arahat).** Moreover, it refers to the **Arana Samadhi** as the zenith of achievement among holy individuals.

depending upon sound, flavor, touch, odour, or any quality. A Bodhisattva should develop a mind which alights *upon nothing whatsoever."*

Historically, the Nikaya Buddhism schools introduced this theology of "personalities" or bodies that lie beyond the five categories of form, feeling, perception, impulse, and consciousness. True stream-winners, or "Strottapanna," comprehend the illusory nature of form, feelings, and perception derived from the senses *and are advised to ignore them.* These sensory inputs were called **Skandhas** or "heaps," referring to groupings of human biological stimulations to phenomena.

Understanding our interaction with phenomena should be a core study and practice of understanding our human condition. Yet, these verses recommend transcending our reactions to phenomena to achieve exalted personages such as **Arahathood, Bodhisattva**, and esoteric states like **Anuttara-Samyak-Sambodhi**, among others.

This perception that humans must circumvent our biological reactions to achieve a disembodied experience is still the primary practice of all spiritual practices in the Far East and Asia. In most forums, gurus preach the gold standard of spirituality of non-duality. It is as if our natural condition is the non-dual state, not our original state that we emerged from into this dualistic incarnation.

The question of where consciousness is experienced has been vitiated by a failure to ask a basic, and possibly obvious question:

If non-duality is the Universe's goal or aspiration, then why was there Evolution in the first place? Why is there so much diversity or duality in the Universe?

This apparent contradiction is puzzling but serves as a starting point for discussing the ancients' lack of knowledge of how our cognitive apparatus generates our embodied experience and our sense of Self and Personhood.

For instance, these verses marginalize, in fact, alienate the role of our cognitive apparatus- the product of 13.5 billion years of evolution - in our understanding of Consciousness or Reality. Our evolutionary journey has equipped us with a diverse set of cognitive tools crucial for finding purpose and fulfillment. Neglecting this aspect undermines the complexity and potential of the human mind and its capacity to form reality.

Further, they also imply that language can accurately define the undefinable. *[This deficiency and limitations of language further contributes to a fractured understanding of the Self and consciousness among religious followers, which I explore in the following section. (Part 2]*

I submit that the original authors of various spiritual texts lacked access to modern experimentation and cognitive science studies. However, such illiteracy should not persist in the 21st century. Almost deliberately, this ignorance is still pervasive. The obsession with achieving supernatural understanding or superhuman qualities, while neglecting our cognitive abilities that allow thought, insight, and personal fulfillment, hinders all spiritual seekers' comprehension of human consciousness and growth.

For instance, our brains are constantly inundated with images, sounds, and smells when we engage with phenomena. The brain, as a recipient of this bombardment, strives to determine plausibility, and achieve coherence and order from the encounter, for the sole purpose of predicting outcomes and determining how to act based on those predictions.

In philosophical terms, we might say that the onslaught of "sight, sound, touch, flavor, smell, or any thought or feeling arising" from that onslaught is phenomenological. Phenomenology describes what we can experience directly, leading to our reactions. For example, stimuli like "this sun feels hot" or "I feel hungry", or if someone cuts us off in traffic, hopefully, you will recognise we respond accordingly.

And yet, the verse suggests that we must ignore the inputs of our faculties and ascend "higher." This raises the question: if we ignore our inputs, how do we interpret the world and arrive at meaning? How do we arrive at insight? How do we make mistakes and grow from learning to insight?

Scientific research and other discoveries reveal that evolutionary biology has shaped us into thinking creatures. This forces us to reframe our understanding of consciousness within our evolutionary arc. Is my conscious expansion independent of my corporeal engagement with the world? How did my evolutionary biology shape my relationship with the world and enable me to perceive my place in it?

Our focus should be on interpreting our 'duality', our diversity, and our epistemic reactions within this diversity and inter-connectedness. The only way we experience consciousness is through experience by our interactions with the external environment.

In essence, the principle of Universal Causality or "Ultimate Reality"—which we neither fully grasp nor control—is generally accepted that life happens *to* us; however, we cannot ignore the fact that we can actively influence our lives by comprehending our embodied consciousness. The core proposition throughout this book is a call for reorienting the conversation towards understanding our embodied consciousness, specifically to understand the fundamental role our cognitive systems play in shaping human perception in our pursuit of meaning and fulfillment.

To underline this proposition, a few notable scientific accomplishments from approximately the last century and a half is certainly worth touching upon. For any ardent student of consciousness, these case studies will be of great interest. They provide ample impetus for the reader to explore new ways of understanding embodiment. Numerous studies in neuroscience and cognitive science are available to expand the reader's understanding of the basis of our personhood and our sense of self in the world.

✳✳✳

In his ground-breaking work **"On the Origin of Species" (1859)**[45], **Charles Darwin** explored the intricate connections between the

---

45.   Darwin, Charles. (1859). On the Origin of Species.

physical and mental aspects of life, suggesting that all living beings evolve through natural selection, affecting both their corporeal and mental endowments. In essence, Darwin describes humans as evolving, cognizing beings struggling to thrive and reproduce in unpredictable conditions[46].

Modern scientists have built upon this foundation, finding evidence that even microbes exhibit behaviour indicative of mental evolution correlating with physical evolution.[47]

The concept of **Umwelt**, first introduced by biologist **Jakob von Uexküll** in 1909[48], describes the unique sensory experiences of an organism as it interacts with its environment. Our bodies and minds have evolved simultaneously through constant interactions with our surroundings. This interaction with the environment lends itself to our subjective experience as an individual or organism and shapes our perceptions, senses, and cognitive abilities. In turn, our cognitive apparatus influences our organism's behaviour, perceptions, and survival. By making sense of our social environment, different individuals may interpret and respond to the same stimuli differently based on their unique intentionality, and cognitive processes[49].

This understanding extends beyond neurological evolution, encompassing aneural evolution and revealing cognitive capacities that emerged before nervous systems appeared on the evolutionary timeline.

One such field of study is Basal Cognition[50] which pursues Darwin's insight that life's 'mental faculties' evolved early with physical embodiment and in parallel with it[51]. Basal cognition examines the potential for

---

46. Ibid

47. Lyon, Pamela. (2006). The biogenic approach to cognition.

48. Ibid

49. Should be Research Papers G. Kriszat, et al

50. Lyon P, Keijzer F, Arendt D, Levin M. Reframing cognition

51. Philosophical Transactions of the Royal Society B: Biological Sciences: Vol 376, No 1821

organisms without brains or even nervous systems to possess capacities for knowing and navigating their surroundings.

Pamela Lyons[52], a researcher in this field, emphasizes the importance of understanding cognition as a means for organisms to navigate their environments to survive, thrive, and reproduce. Pamela defines cognition as *"the means by which organisms become familiar with, value, exploit, and evade features of their surroundings in order to survive, thrive, and reproduce"*[53]. This biogenic approach places the source of cognition in the biological mode of existence, rather than limiting it to a neurological or cerebral one.

These studies have demonstrated that cognitive operations typically attributed to brains are, in fact, observed in living forms without brains or neurons. This finding supports Darwin's thesis that the appearance of design in nature requires no designer, divine or otherwise[54] Although some studies may not agree with Darwin's linear model, most scientists do accept his basic premise[55].

A study by neuroscientist **Humberto Maturana** further emphasizes the biological basis of cognition, describing life as self-producing (autopoiesis)[56] rather than merely self-organizing or self-maintaining. Imagine a Tesla factory capable of governing itself, sourcing materials, organizing supply chains, and regenerating resources to produce cars non-stop. Such a system would embody the concept of autopoiesis – a self-producing intelligence exhibited by all cellular life without the need for an external contractor[57].

Don Hoffman, a cognitive scientist, has proposed a theory of consciousness known as "conscious realism," which challenges the

52. Lyon, Pamela. (2006). Philosophical Transactions of the Royal Society B: Biological Sciences: Vol 376, No 1821

53. Ibid

54. Ibid

55. Ibid

56. https://en.wikipedia.org/wiki/Autopoiesis

57. Autopoiesis and Cognition: The Realization of the Living | SpringerLink

traditional view that our perception of reality is a direct representation of the external world. Instead, Hoffman suggests that our experience of reality is more like a virtual reality, created by the brain. He argues that the brain constructs a simplified and functional model of the world, rather than a complete and accurate one, because of evolutionary pressures that prioritize survival over accuracy.[58]

This simplified model of reality can be compared to the experience of coming across a waterfall while thirsty. We only take in the amount of water necessary to quench our thirst, and the rest is never collected because, we would not even see the remaining water cascading down! Similarly, our brain constructs a simplified model of the world that is functional for our survival, but not necessarily a complete or accurate representation of reality.[59]

Anil Seth, another cognitive scientist, has proposed a theory of consciousness called the "predictive processing framework," which similarly challenges the traditional view of consciousness as a passive reflection of the external world. According to this theory, the brain is constantly generating predictions about the world based on prior experiences and sensory input. These predictions are then compared to incoming sensory information, and any discrepancies are used to update the brain's model of the world, resulting in our conscious experience.[60]

Anil Seth's theory of consciousness emphasizes that the experience of being a living organism is what forms the basis of conscious selfhood. He argues that it's more accurate to say that we "are a body" rather than just "have a body". This viewpoint emphasizes the importance of considering *both* the cognitive and physical aspects of our being when studying consciousness.

---

58. Hoffman, D. D. (2012). Conscious realism and the mind-body problem. Mind and Matter, 10(2), 291-328

59. Ibid

60. Seth, A. K. (2013). Interoceptive inference, emotion, and the embodied self. Trends in cognitive sciences, 17(11), 565-573.

To support his theory, Seth points to the fact that our subjective experience of the world is heavily influenced by our physical states and surroundings. For example, when we are hungry, thirsty, or in pain our internal state is quite different from when we are well-fed, hydrated, and comfortable. This suggests that our bodily experiences play a significant role in shaping our consciousness.

Seth's theory also has implications for how we understand the relationship between mind and body. Rather than seeing them as separate entities, he suggests that they are deeply intertwined, with the body providing the foundation for our subjective experience of the world.

Overall, Seth's theory of consciousness emphasizes the importance of taking a holistic view of our being when studying consciousness. By recognizing the role of our physical experiences and surroundings, we can gain a more complete understanding of what it means to be conscious[61].

Both Hoffman and Seth's theories suggest that our conscious experience is actively construed by the brain and influenced by both bottom-up sensory input and top-down predictions and expectations. This challenges the traditional view of our consciousness as a reflection of Universal Consciousness and instead *suggests that our perception of reality is shaped by factors such as our evolutionary history, prior experiences, and expectations.*[62]

Essentially, our consciousness is rooted in our embodiment as living beings.

In the context of *Umwelt*, the subjective experience of an individual or organism is shaped by its perceptions, senses, and cognitive abilities. Hoffman and Seth's theories are consistent with this idea, as they suggest that *our perception of reality is actively constructed by the brain based on*

---

61.   Seth, A. (2019). The bodily basis of consciousness. The Psychologist, 32, 26-29
62.   Hoffman, D. D. (2019). The case against reality: Why evolution hid the truth from our eyes. WW Norton & Company.

sensory input, expectations, and prior experiences, which in turn shape our subjective experience of the world.[63]

Overall, the theories of Hoffman and Seth challenge traditional views of consciousness and provide important insights into the nature of subjective experience and the role of the brain in shaping our perception of the world[64].

As we continue to uncover the mysteries of cognition and consciousness, we must be mindful of the intricate interplay between our corporeal and mental endowments. The exploration of this connection will undoubtedly illuminate our understanding of what it means to be a living organism and a conscious being in an ever-evolving universe. We should be awestruck at the progress of Homo sapiens over the past 13.5 billion years, one can only wonder how much more we might evolve in the next 13.5 billion years as our environment continues to change.

Further, a vital operation of our cognitive processes is language. Language plays a significant role in shaping our understanding of personhood and consciousness as we interact with the environment and others. However, the limitations of the language alongside our prediction engine further exacerbate a fractured concept of ourselves. *(More of this deficiency of language in the next chapter).*

Many proponents of Buddhism argue that verses these only caution against the dangers of "clinging" to our sensations, which they believe is the root cause of our suffering or *"dukkha."* However, I respectfully disagree with this perspective, which I believe is naive and indicative of a simplistic understanding of the human mind.

In my opinion, most people do not have a static relationship to their sensations. Instead, our bodies immediately process these inputs leading to interoception and perception, to keep you alive and well.

---

63.   Umwelt. (2021, January 16). In Wikipedia. Retrieved March 29, 2023, from https://en.wikipedia.org/wiki/Umwelt.

64.   Seth, A. K. (2013). Interoceptive inference, emotion, and the embodied self. Trends in cognitive sciences, 17(11), 565-573.

Sermonizing that humans should not cling to sensations when we do not, in fact, cling to them, creates a false narrative that deflects attention away from the true causative value of our brains and sensory inputs in creating our perceptions. Our suffering or *dukkha* arises from our cognitive machinery's inability to make sense of the onslaught of information we face in our lives to arrive at actionable insight, not from any supposed clinging to sensations.

Circumventing our Embodied Consciousness and examining how our cognitive apparatus works is the Un-Being of You.

Our perceptions are not limited to our personal experiences but also include our interactions with others in our social and cultural environment. It is through these transpersonal interactions with our families, communities, and society that we develop our perceptions of personhood. Without these interactions that form our cognitive framework, there can be no *gestalt*, no sense of being, or, as Anil Seth aptly titled his book, "**Being You**[65]."

This *umwelt*, which shapes our conscious experience, is constantly trying to keep pace with a shape shifting Universe.

To deepen our understanding of consciousness, we must shift our perspective and recognize the profound implications of our biological evolution on the content and causality of our cognition. This requires re-centreing our understanding of consciousness around the corporeal and our biological reflexes.

❋❋❋

Even in the 21st century, there are those who defend the horrific practice of Female Genital Mutilation, (FGM) believing it to be necessary for controlling a woman's sexuality. More sinisterly, some claim that allowing women to feel sexual pleasure will open the door to the Devil!

A dogma rooted in misogyny, which suppresses women's inherent rights to sexual pleasure and ecstasy, should act as a cautionary signpost for any ideology aiming to disregard our sensory experiences as the basis of our comprehension of nature. By denying us the experience of embodied consciousness, such ideologies do nothing but impede our true expansion.

When I hear a self-proclaimed guru espousing the platitude, "*We are not the body, we are not the mind,*", I recognize my initial reception of their message is through my sensory perception first. This sensory input is subsequently processed by my cognitive faculties to derive significance and relevance in my life. Ultimately, it is through the experiential lens of my physical being that I become aware of consciousness and must therefore strive to gain control over it.

Recognizing and understanding my cognitive processes paves the way for profound insight into the significance and mastery of my existence.

---

65. Seth, A. (2018). Being You: A New Science of Consciousness. The MIT Press.

Chapter 9

Words Mean Nothing, because Words Turn Back.

(CONTINUATION OF SECTION 9,10)

VERSE 10: SETTING FORTH PURE LANDS

Buddha said: Subhuti, what do you think? In the remote past when the Tathagata was with Dipankara Buddha, did he have any degree of attainment in the Good Law? No, World honoured One. When the Tathagata was with Dipankara Buddha he had no degree of attainment in the Good Law. Subhuti, what do you think? Does a Bodhisattva set forth any majestic Buddhalands? No, World-honoured One.

Wherefore? Because setting forth majestic Buddha-lands is not a majestic setting forth; this is merely a name. [Then Buddha continued:] Therefore, Subhuti, all Bodhisattvas, lesser and great, should develop a pure, lucid mind, not depending upon sound, flavor, touch, odour, or any quality. A Bodhisattva should develop a mind which alights upon no thing whatsoever; and so should he establish it. Subhuti, this may be likened to a human frame as large as the mighty Mount Sumeru. What do you think? Would such a body be great? Subhuti replied: Great indeed, World-honoured One. This is because Buddha has explained that no body is called a great body

In the previous verse of the Diamond Sutra, there's an intriguing invitation to distance ourselves from sensory experiences and delve into a realm that goes beyond our physical existence. This notion isn't exclusive to this sacred text; it is a common theme echoing through many spiritual traditions.

Nevertheless, we need to ask ourselves a vital question: How can we meditate or reflect upon any concept that we have no experience, understanding, or comprehension of?

This question might unsettle some or clash with their beliefs, and to those, I suggest they consider not proceeding further. Yet for others, this question bears significant importance and warrants further scrutiny.

In this chapter, I hope to address the mereological confusion[66] by demagogues who imply language can serve as a surrogate for describing the inexpressible and Universal Consciousness. The inadequacy of language in ancient so-called sacred texts has gone unanswered, and I do submit this has fragmented and misled many in their comprehension of Consciousness and Reality.

Recalling the first section of these two verses that enumerates the sensory inputs we should not cling to, it states, "All Bodhisattvas, lesser and great, should cultivate a pure, lucid mind, independent of sound, flavor, touch, odour, or any quality. A Bodhisattva should foster a mind that alights upon nothing whatsoever."

These five sensory inputs allude to and are classified as the Skandhas[67], which explain how humans conceptualize and perceive the world. In the understanding of the ancients, our eyes discern visual stimuli, leading to the taxonomy Skandhas of form, feeling, perception, mental formations, and consciousness. For example, our ears detect sound, our nose discerns smell, our tongue identifies taste, and our body senses touch, all of which the ancients categorized as the Skandhas.

---

66. Mereological confusion is a philosophical term that refers to a type of misunderstanding related to the relationships between parts and wholes. "Mereology" is the study of these part-whole relationships.

67. Five skandhas - Encyclopedia of Buddhism

Aiming for a deeper comprehension of the Skandhas' categorization that attempts to tether concepts to labels, I was drawn to their similarities with the Koshas[68], in the Upanishads which portray our Being as sheaths.

The Skandhas, or five aggregates, provide a framework for comprehending the components of human experience in Buddhism, while the Koshas, or five sheaths, derived from the Skandhas, offer a way of understanding the layers of human consciousness in Hinduism. The correspondence between both is generally considered unmistakable.

Even the most cursory exploration of both the Skandhas and the Koshas reveals how their classification systems, coupled to their reliance on language to conceptualize the world, can inadvertently contribute to this mereological fallacy.

So, what conclusions can we draw from the Skandhas and the Koshas?

The Skandhas and Koshas serve as vital frameworks in Indian philosophy, utilizing semantics to categorize diverse aspects of human experience and existence. This approach reflects the intricate relationship between language and the understanding of reality in early Indian thought. In the nascent days of philosophy on the Indian subcontinent, language was instrumental in comprehending and interpreting the world. Philosophers and scholars from various schools of thought employed language to conceptualize reality, articulate ideas, and participate in intellectual debates. Even today, with two people sharing a cup of *chai*, we will have philosophy!

In the case of the Skandhas, the Buddhist tradition delineates a comprehensive taxonomy of human experience. Similarly, the Koshas in the Vedantic tradition offer an all-encompassing semantic framework for understanding human existence. The five sheaths present a hierarchical categorization, with each layer representing a subtler aspect of the Self. The use of language in this context enabled philosophers to express a complex model of the human being, connecting the physical, energetic, mental, intellectual, and spiritual dimensions. By employing taxonomies and categorizations, these frameworks allowed scholars to dissect and

---

68. Koshas: What These 5 Layers Mean in Eastern Philosophy (healthline.com)

explore various aspects of human experience, shaping the way people conceptualized the self and the world around them.

Indeed, language serves as a means of expressing the ancient's understanding of the world and their comprehension of what ultimate Reality may mean. This perspective of communicating Reality is pervasive across religious societies, as early thought pioneers realized that we cannot think of, discuss, or conceive the world without a tool, which is language. However, the traditional view of language and grammar as independent of meaning or intent is limited, as it suggests that our theatre that forms our thoughts can be described using formal logic and taxonomy, such as the Skandhas and Koshas. As I introduced in the previous chapter, the philosophers' thesis on consciousness believed that language and thought were built on a system of logical propositions, with a perfect correspondence between the structure of the proposition and the structure of the world and reality!

Here, I offer a perspective that challenges the traditional view that nominal names proposition represent universal concepts. My perspective asserts that our cognition arises from an action-oriented engagement with the world and society, which emphasizes the importance of context and subjective experience in shaping our understanding of concepts. By recognizing the dynamic and evolving nature of our cognitive processes, we can better appreciate the complexities of language that arrive at meaning and the ways in which they are intertwined with our perceptions and interactions with the world around us.

This embodied cognition and consciousness approach posited by scholars like George Lakoff, Rafael Núñez, and Shaun Gallagher emphasizes the importance of the body and physical experience in shaping our cognitive processes. Referencing mathematics, George Lakoff and Rafael Nunez argue in their book "Where Mathematics Comes From" that our understanding of abstract mathematical concepts is largely metaphorical and grounded in our sensory-motor experiences[69]. They contend that mathematical concepts (that we

---

69. Lakoff, G., & Nunez, R. E. (2001). Where Mathematics Comes From: How the Embodied Mind Brings Mathematics into Being. New York: Basic Books.

normally consider fixed or finite) are not innate or universal, but rather emerge from our bodily experiences and cultural practices. Lakoff and Nunez's thesis challenges traditional views of mathematics as a purely logical and formal system and has important implications for the way we teach and learn mathematics[70]. Their view challenges traditional linguistic and taxonomic frameworks like the Skandas and Koshas as well, which are often criticized for obscuring important differences and nuances between concepts and perspectives that differ between individuals derived from meaning and intentionality.[71.]

While taxonomies and categorization systems provide us with nominal names which may be necessary for clear communication and understanding in many fields, including science and medicine, they should not be viewed as the ultimate representation of the world and consciousness. Instead, our understanding of the world and ourselves should emerge from direct experience and physical engagement with the environment.

Focusing on a single category from the Skandhas and their corresponding Koshas as an example, can reveal the perceptual barriers that hinder religious followers from comprehending their epistemic awareness and self in relation to the world.

Let us consider the first Skandha, Rupa, which pertains to Form and Food, and its parallel in the Upanishads, Anna-Maya Kosha.

Both the Skandhas and the Koshas elucidate our understanding of the human body through form, and how our conceptual impressions arise by labelling forms and objects. Buddhist texts use Rupa to encompass all physical phenomena, referring to everything we can touch, hear, see, smell, and taste. Intriguingly, Rupa does not merely denote the practitioner's body but categorizes the sensory inputs that inform us of our body. In other words, Rupa does not convey the intuitive notion that

70. Lakoff, G. (2008). The Political Mind: A Cognitive Scientist's Guide to Your Brain and Its Politics. New York: Viking.

71. A Brief Guide to Embodied Cognition: Why You Are Not Your Brain - Scientific American Blog Network

the body processes its senses, instead, it is the senses that possess the body!

The corresponding layer to Rupa in the Koshas is Anna-Maya Kosha or the food sheath, a more fitting term. However, as previously mentioned, the application of taxonomy of nominal names that purport to describe the world mistakenly attributes objects with the qualities that allegedly give rise to our perceptions.

For instance, when one claims that milk is white or fire is hot, do these attributes belong to the objects or the Experiencer? This notion, which refers to essential qualities or attributes inseparable from an object, comes from the Vedanta philosophy and the concept known as "Guna".

Sri Shankaracharya used analogies of the whiteness of milk and or heat of fire to illustrate the concept of "Guna". The concept plays a crucial role in proposing the nature of ultimate reality, as well as the world and the individual self. In the vast and hair-splitting tapestry of Vedanta philosophy, the concept of "Guna" tethers the object and its attributes into an inseparable unity.

The "Guna" concept seems to imply that an object's attributes are fixed and objective, an irrefutable fact. This philosophical system starkly overlooks the observer's subjectivity and personal experience, a source of human perception that is inherently unpredictable. By not delineating the object from its attributes, this concept neglects the diverse range of individual interpretations that arise from one's distinct background, beliefs, and cognitive processes, which shape our unique perspectives of the world and our sense of Personhood.

Keen observers of human experience will note that our perception of objective reality is far from static. Our senses and cognitive processes act as mediators, and perhaps even arbiters, of our understanding. Consequently, our experience of an object's attributes is subject to the inexorable influence of personal biases, limitations, and the cultural context in which we find ourselves immersed. The direct experience framework, in contrast, underscores the importance of the experiencer's active participation in the process of perception and understanding. It is the experiencer who experiences the white of the milk or the heat of the fire. We could ask: What's the colour of milk through the compound eyes of a housefly as it alights on a bowl?

The ever-changing landscape of human perception is not wholly captured by the rigid confines of the "Guna" concept which attaches the attribute to the object and separates the experience of the Experiencer.

This misunderstanding forms the cornerstone of many people's misconception that Consciousness and The Self are also Objects that can be defined and reified. This view becomes accentuated in the second description of sañña-khandha and mano-maya kosha (the mental sheath of perception).

The Pali literature elaborates on how we conceptualize by nominally naming objects, in the way we sense colours. The Sunna (s)Khanda goes on to describe language as the way we name objects, stating "Therefore, things arise." To quote: "And why do you call it 'perception'? Because it perceives, thus it is called 'perception.' What does it perceive? It perceives blue, it perceives yellow, it perceives red, it perceives white. Because it perceives, it is called perception."

This brings me to the crux of my disagreement with those who advocate a simplistic view of perception, equating our sensory faculties with the totality of understanding. Vision is not the same as insight. Our senses gather data from independent sources like eyes, ears, and touch. After these various inputs impinge on our brain, and they impinge at different times, only then does our brain combine these inputs to confirm the plausibility and *relevance* of the phenomenon we are witnessing.

The assumption that sight and perception are synonymous betrays a shallow appreciation of the rich tapestry that constitutes human cognition. It is the duty of any thoughtful person to probe further and disentangle the intricate threads that weave together our faculties, epistemic experiences, and the enigmatic realm of subjective consciousness.

Sight, while undoubtedly significant, merely captures the visual aspect of the world and translates it into images for our cognitive consumption. Perception, a far more complex phenomenon, melds the melange of sensory input from sight, hearing, touch, taste, and smell, conducting a symphony of cognitive processes to create a coherent and meaningful understanding of our environment. To equate sight with perception is to mistake a single instrument for the orchestra itself.

The pursuit of epistemic experience requires delving into the complex labyrinth of human cognition, where knowledge and comprehension arise from the amalgamation of observation, reason, and experience. Perception plays a pivotal role in this process, providing the raw materials for our cognitive faculties to work upon. However, it is but one component of the intricate process of knowledge acquisition, which necessitates critical thinking, evidence evaluation, and the refinement of prediction, ultimately culminating in comprehension and insight.

The subjective experience occupies a murky realm where qualia, the indescribable qualities of consciousness, hold sway. While perception serves as the starting point, the subjective experience comprises a multifaceted array of emotions, memories, personal beliefs, and individual perspectives. These diverse elements intermingle and converge to form our one-of-a-kind consciousness.

Equating the data obtained through our sensory organs with perception would amount to an egregious oversimplification, an affront to the intellectual and intuitive complexities of human understanding. To navigate the labyrinthine corridors of human understanding and insight, one must recognize the intricate interplay of these elements. Perception, far from being the sole determinant, provides the foundation for both our epistemic and subjective experiences. Our cognitive faculties, in concert with our personal histories and individual perspectives, transform sensory data into meaningful beliefs and understanding. The delicate interplay of perception, cognition, and subjective experience ultimately illuminates the path to actionable insight.

Allow me to share a personal story that highlights the difference between our sensory input and the more intricate realms of perception and understanding derived from nominal labels we incorrectly term as reality.

In January 2022, I awoke from a medically induced coma in the ICU, immediately finding myself incapable of forming words or language. I was a body with faculties, assaulted by sights and sounds, yet unable to comprehend their meaning. My eyes saw water jugs, tables, and nurses, but these were mere pixels on my retina, devoid of meaning.

My eyes were just lenses of a camera, capturing images without the ability to interpret or understand them. As days passed, my cognitive processes began to return, and my language skills slowly returned. From simple labels or nominal names, like "jug, water, nurse" my brain extrapolated and allowed me to communicate with the nurse, transforming those labels to communicate meaning; for instance, "I am thirsty."

This intense experience taught me the difference between the raw data gathered by our senses and the cognitive apparatus within me that transmutes mere data and information into meaning, shaping our perceptions and perspectives. Experiencing that my cognitive processes were deeply rooted in my physical self, I discovered that my body's sensory organs was vital when interacting with the world and my cognitive faculties were essential for decision-making and action.

After my discharge, I gained a profound appreciation for those with visual or hearing impairments and how they construct their reality through their body's heightened awareness of their surroundings.

Considering my experience, it became starkly clear that equating sensory faculties with perception oversimplifies the complex, interconnected processes leading to understanding and insight. It is the delicate balance between our senses, cognitive faculties, and personal experiences that ultimately enables us to navigate the world with wisdom and depth.

Going further, in the Taittiriya Upanishad, the concept of *mano-maya-kosha*, the sheath of the mind, transcends mere object labelling and nominal names. It explores specific applications of language, such as Vedic chants and proper grammar in the Vedas, to represent and engage with universal consciousness. While many argue that these rites and chants represent a connection with the Cosmos, I contend that without the cognitive processes arising from our embodied and enacted engagements, these activities remain mechanical and leave the individual's life sterile.

We recognize both Rupa skandhas and the Mano-maya-kosha emphasize language as the primary tool representing our environment, enabling us to engage with our surroundings.

However, our ancestors were presented with a complex challenge when trying to deconstruct language when trying to align meaning and intent with experience. They subtly hinted at this quandary in an intriguing verse found just a few lines later in the **Taittiriya Upanishad**.

The ancient thinkers had an innate understanding of the essence of consciousness, but due to the inherent deficiency of language and semantics to describe our epistemic awareness and subjective relationship to the phenomena, they were unable to articulate their insights adequately. This has resulted in an unbridgeable gap or an incomplete understanding of reality and consciousness to the worshipful faithful, which persists to this day. They realized attempts to define consciousness were futile and will always be limited if we continue to rely solely on attempts at definition and reification.

Consider Just a few verses later in the Taittreya Upanishad, the ancients hint at the limitations of language in capturing the essence of human understanding.

The verse states:

"Before they reach it, words turn back together with the mind; One who knows that bliss of Brahman, he is never afraid (TU 2. 3,9)."

So, why should words turn back? What does that mean?

Brahman is described as *"That which is unspeakable, unperceivable, and unknowable"*. In other words, it is the antithesis of form. Instead of "formless," the term "Un-Formable" may be more appropriate.

Attempting to concretize an experience that defies quantification amounts to reducing the irreducible through definitions. Can we quantify a subjective experience? Can the Un-Formable, Brahman, be reduced to form?

Nagarjuna's frequently cited analogy of fire and fuel highlights the interdependency of objects or things. As he astutely points out, fire cannot exist without another element—fuel—which, in turn, cannot burn without air, which also depends on something else, and so forth. Yet, he employs infinite linear regression to conclude that there is no object or thing at infinity and, therefore, arrives at Shunyata.

How can we have *relationships* with objects and then assert there is no object? This is a prime example of materialism, which claims that Shunyata somehow is a derivative of objects and labels. I consider this Nagarjuna's half-truth.

This enigma will continue to mystify us if we attempt to label our Personhood as if it were a concrete object devoid of our subjectivity and indescribable experiences derived from engaging with our environment of objects and things. Like Anil Seth proposes "we are a body, not that we possess a body". If we try to define our Self in concrete terms, then indeed, we are no-THING, *but that is not the same as declaring we are nothing.*

In the previous chapters, I introduced a few studies in cognitive science and evolutionary biology that discussed our sense of Personhood and consciousness is not solely a product of the brain. It also arises from the interdependency between the brain and the body, as well as our interactions with the environment that shape our perspectives and cognitive reflexes.

Our understanding of consciousness and reality is shaped by the intricate dance between our sensory input, cognitive processes, and personal experiences. Modern cognitive science underscores the limitations of probing human consciousness. To explore the mysteries of consciousness, we would have to appreciate the interdependencies and complexities that underpin our perceptions and perspectives.

Misunderstandings can occur due to the limitations and nuances of language, which endeavours to mirror our private theatre of thought, which are subject to infinite interpretations and meanings. We constantly try to make sense of reality through the lens of our subjective experiences, which are often difficult to express through conventional language.

When words meet the indescribable or, our subjective inner theatre, that is where "Words Turn Back."

In the immortal words of Shakespeare's Romeo and Juliet, Juliet muses, "What's in a name? That which we call a rose, by any other name would smell as sweet." This sentiment holds true when referring to objects but becomes more complex when pondering our relationships and interactions with others, such as our bipolar Aunt Rose or our crazy cousin Rose.

Noam Chomsky's theory of language[72] posited language and grammar as an autonomous entity separate from semantics fits well into our discussion comparing the taxonomy of Skandhas and Koshas. It was a view of language in which grammar was independent of meaning or communication and has close echoes to our ancient forebears of the use of nominal labels to describe reality.

His view limits our understanding of language and its role in human communication and culture. Chomsky's ideas were formulated during a time when computer science and artificial intelligence were nascent fields, and these ideas seem to be gaining new traction with the advent of AI chatbots and their seeming sentient responses.

The principles underlying both AI coding and textual canons converge on the assumption that a universal grammar can distill the aspects of human existence and reality into measurable metrics.

Communication is not simply a matter of following a pre-existing set of rules, but rather a complex and dynamic process that is shaped by social, cultural, and environmental factors.

❋❋❋

---

72. **Noam Chomsky's Language Acquisition Theory:** Noam Chomsky's Language Acquisition Theory - Free Essay Example - Edubirdie

When contemplating the limits of language and the potential for AI sentience, we must consider the difference between real-world experiences and simulated experiences.

While working on the chatbot LaMDA[73,] Blake Lemoine's claimed that AI was sentient. On the face of it, the output seemed to display a level of self-awareness[74.] This certainly merited a closer examination of AI sentience because it spooked some who viewed the transcript of the conversation. To be fair, that claim did not pass the sentient test right at the beginning. AI's seemingly human-like output is achieved through artificial neural networks and massive computational power that trawls archived human responses and spits out the best answer to the question from its learned interactions with humans.

As we delve into the intricacies of language and our interplay with reality, we must also acknowledge the influence of symbols, metaphors, and myths in sculpting and communicate our experiences. We seldom acknowledge the role that implied communication like body language holds in our societal interactions. These forms of expression, although they often fall short of encapsulating the profundity of our subjective experiences, present a vivid mosaic for attempting to articulate meaning and intent.

---

73. Language Model for Dialogue Applications.

74. Google AI Chatbot Interview Transcript: What Did LaMDA Say to Blake Lemoine? - Bloomberg

With the emergence of AI and it's escalating prowess in language processing, it is imperative that we harbour a discerning scepticism towards the concept of artificial sentience. As AI continues to advance, we may become increasingly vulnerable to information distortion through deep fake videos and voice imitations. Astonishingly, our future President or Prime Minister might turn out to be an AI bot!

I stand firm in my conviction that AI will never achieve sentience, arguing that without consciousness or self-awareness, no computer can be genuinely sentient. While AI language skills are advancing at an impressive pace, it does not imply the development of sentience. AI can simulate human dialogue and produce responses that seem self-aware, but true sentience necessitates a level of understanding and experiential depth that surpasses sheer computational capabilities.

To qualify as sentient, it is necessary for an entity not just to engage in interactive phenomena, but also to infuse them with meaning and intent, and to generate spontaneous qualia from these encounters. Intimacy is vital. AI can effectively solve predefined complex problems, yet it will never be able to identify a problem based on the unique human interpretation and intentionality of a situation.

For example, An AI, working on bridge construction, can efficiently process complex mathematical data and provide optimal solutions within predefined parameters. However, it lacks the broader understanding that comes from human sentience.

A human engineer, on the other hand, can consider a wider range of factors beyond just mathematical equations, such as aesthetics, community impact, and future developments. They also think creatively and laterally when unexpected problems arise, guided by intuition and experience. Moreover, a human understands the bridge's purpose and value at a deeper level, seeing it as a connection between communities and a facilitator of development, not just a mathematical problem.

While AI has computational capabilities that excel in processing and solving predefined problems, human sentience brings a richer understanding, creative thinking, and a wider perspective to problem-solving, which is beyond the reach of AI.

As we grapple with these questions, we should remain open to the possibility that the limits of language may ultimately be transcended by our innate human capacity for empathy, creativity, and understanding.

Ultimately, whether we delve into the timeless writings of Shakespeare, engage with the profound theories of Noam Chomsky, or grapple with the challenges presented by AI, we must continuously underscore the significance of cultivating our unique viewpoints, experiences, and comprehension. It is through these pursuits that we unlock a deeper appreciation for the intricate beauty of life and treasure the boundless opportunities nested within the spectrum of human experience.

One of the beautiful examples of a character who eulogized Embodied Consciousness in the 'here and now' was **Roy McBride** in the movie **Ad Astra.**

Perhaps you too could relate to his words.

"'I'm unsure of the future, but I'm not concerned. I will rely on those closest to me, and I will share their burdens, as they share mine. I will live and love.'

Ready to do my job to the best of my abilities. I am focused only on the essentials, to the exclusion of all else. I will make only pragmatic decisions. I will not allow myself to be distracted. I will not allow my mind to linger on that which is unimportant. I will not rely on anyone or anything. I will not be vulnerable to mistakes. Resting BPM, forty-seven. Submit."

Chapter 10

Those who Worship don't Know, those that Know, don't Worship.
(Verses 11-12)

VERSE 11: THE SUPERIORITY OF UNFORMULATED TRUTH

Subhuti, if there were as many Ganges rivers as the sand grains of the Ganges, would the sand-grains of them all bemany? Subhuti said: Many indeed, World-honoured One! Even the Ganges rivers would be innumerable; how much more so would be their sand-grains? Subhuti, I will declare a truth to you. If a good man or good woman filled three thousand galaxies of worlds with the seven treasures for each sand-grain in all those Ganges rivers, and gave all away in gifts of alms, would he gain great merit? Subhuti answered: Great indeed, World-honoured One! Then Buddha declared: Nevertheless, Subhuti, if a good man or good woman studies this Discourse only so far as to receive and retain four lines, and teaches and explains them to others, the consequent merit would be far greater.

and

VERSE 12: VENERATION OF THE TRUE DOCTRINE

Furthermore, Subhuti, you should know that wheresoever this Discourse is proclaimed, by even so little as four lines, that place should be venerated by the whole realms of Gods, Men and Titans as though it were a Buddha-Shrine. How much more is this so in the case of one who is able to receive and retain the whole and read and recite it throughout! Subhuti, you should know that such a one attains the highest and most wonderful truth. Wheresoever this sacred Discourse may be found there should you comport yourself as though in the presence of Buddha and disciples worthy of honour.

A substantial part of the Diamond Sutra consistently revisits its core teachings, advocating ethical practices and recognizing the sutra as a stupa that contains Buddha Himself. These concepts, despite subtle variations, is reiterated in this verse too, necessitating a somewhat nuanced perspective for its interpretation.

In this chapter, I will return to the phrase, "repeating just four lines..." This phrase serves as a potent reminder of the Diamond Sutra's mission to propagate its teachings and emphasizes the crucial role of ethical adherence. Moreover, I will reference other pivotal passages in the Sutra, requesting your patience as I underscore these concepts with slightly different perspectives.

Those who worship don't know, those that know, don't worship.

Bodhidharma[75] was a semi-legendary figure, who emerged six centuries post-Pali Canon and during a resurgent Hindu era. He is known for introducing Chan Buddhism, the precursor to Zen, and held highly critical views towards the reliance on texts and submission to external authority when pursuing spiritual discipline. His apocryphal anecdotes and quotes vividly underscore his emphasis on introspection, suggesting that he favoured inner exploration over the veneration of objects and texts. This famous quote attributed to **Bodhidharma**, one might assume that the veneration of Buddha or any other religious figure would have ceased then and there. But it was not to be.

---

75. Bodhidharma - Wikipedia

As previously noted in my introductory chapter, no belief system, philosophical doctrine, or countercultural movement arises in isolation. The 6th century AD was a time of great philosophical and religious foment in Northern India. The Gupta Empire, which had ruled over much of the subcontinent for over 200 years, had collapsed, and its territory was divided into several smaller kingdoms. These kingdoms were home to a wide variety of religious and philosophical traditions, including various branches of Hinduism and Jainism aside from Buddhism. Not unexpectedly, debates raged between these various religions and schools[76].

---

76. The Oxford History of Hinduism." by Arvind Sharma (1999); "The Hindu World." by Heinrich Zimmer (1956)

Bodhidharma emerged from this milieu defined by the spiritual resurgence of the priestly class and the turmoil of war[77], a period that fostered a deep-seated desire among the common people to establish a connection with and invoke the power of cosmic forces.

Given the fierce competition among ideologies during the time of the Buddha, the authors of the Diamond Sutra, as marketing virtuosos, recognized the potential for these texts to become the viral social media of their day. The Diamond Sutra composition is akin to a scripted dialogue between a ventriloquist and their puppet, engaging the audience with a conversational style that lay people could more easily absorb than the formidable Vedas.

Thus, the Buddha character asserts that future audiences would reap immense merit by accepting the text's spiritually liberating effects. In this way, the copied text could proliferate as effectively as modern social media.

The Diamond Sutra's emphasis on the power of merely reading four lines serves as a formidable tool for proselytization, surpassing even the Christian directive to *"go ye forth and preach the gospel to every creature[78]"*. Ergo, any reader of the Diamond Sutra does not require a missionary to decipher or understand the Diamond Sutra; simply reading four lines could lead to Nirvana.

Much of the text reiterates this promotional message, increasingly emphasizing the idea of venerating the Buddha within the text, rather than shunning idol worship. This imbues the text with a sanctity that the great Bodhidharma would likely disdain.

Considering the Vedas and their associated rites were beyond the reach of the common folk, a text claiming that reciting just four lines would grant access to Nirvana might be likened to receiving spiritual cheat codes for salvation. Combined with this edict to recite just 4 lines, The Diamond Sutra shifted the focus from inaccessible external deities

---

77.   Ibid

78.   The Book of St. Mark, 16:15

to the personal effort of ethics, placing the power to shape their spiritual destiny firmly within their control.

This revolutionary approach presented an inclusive path to spiritual growth, the Diamond Sutra facilitated the expansion of Buddhism and its ideas among a wider range of individuals.

The consequence of a freely available text like the Diamond Sutra served not only as a spiritual guide but also as an instrument of social change, disrupting the status quo and challenging the religious establishment. However, it is essential to recognize the inherent contradiction in the text's simultaneous promotion of formlessness, and at the same time its exhortation to revere the Buddha within the text.

The text becomes akin to a stupa containing all Buddhas, heavenly gods, and demi-gods. This call to idolize the Buddha and the text stands in contrast with the initial portions of the Diamond Sutra, which emphasize that the Tathagata and all beings are already liberated. The text now transforms into an object of worship, rather than a subject of reflection, or interpretation.

Bodhidharma, the great thinker who expanded Chan Buddhism in China, disdained such veneration of texts and external objects. It is crucial to acknowledge the critical thinkers like Bodhidharma who guided aspirants away from the stagnation of text worship and mere proselytization. They challenged dogma and encouraged introspection.

One might question whether Bodhidharma was a Buddhist in the conventional or religious sense, and if Chan Buddhism is indeed related to traditional Buddhism because, unlike the myriad schools that studied the texts for the text's sake, Bodhidharma's teachings emphasized the importance of looking directly at the mind rather than relying on hearsay that cannot describe the ineffable. One would say these were the early days of clinical psychology in the Far East.

The crux of his teachings lies in the first two verses of the **Lankavatara Sutra**, a challenging text to read of a dialogue between the character of the Buddha and *Mahamati*

As discussed in a previous chapter, " Words Mean Nothing Because Words Turn Back," Bodhidharma argues that the only experience of our true original nature cannot be found in words and letters. Instead, he directs attention to our first-hand experience or what he refers to as "The Mind[79]."

D.T. Suzuki explains that the recurrent theme of the Lankavatara Sutra is the deficiency of language or words to express ultimate reality.

In the Lankavatara Sutra, the character of the Buddha asserts:

"If, Mahamati, you say that because of the reality of words the objects are, this talk lacks in sense. Words are not known in all the Buddha-lands; words, Mahamati, are an artificial creation. In some Buddha-lands, ideas are indicated by looking steadily, in others by gestures, in still others by a frown, by the movement of the eyes, by laughing, by yawning, or by the clearing of the throat, or by recollection, or by trembling."

In contrast to the ineffectiveness of words, the Sutra emphasizes the importance of "self-realization" attained through insight , which occurs "when one has an insight into reality as it is"[80.] This truth is beyond categories of discrimination, referring to the human tendency to choose one thing over another, or by defining and labelling subjective experiences, due to personal bias stemming from their conditioning.

The teachings of Bodhidharma was neatly paraphrased by another great Zen Master **Shunryu Suzuki**, he says: " *The purpose of studying Buddhism is not to study Buddhism, but to study ourselves"*.

I couldn't agree more with this quote. Regardless of whether it's Advaita, Gnosticism, Hermeticism, Sufism, or any other such teachings, the essential understanding is that their purpose is to aid us in comprehending ourselves through experience. Recognizing this is true freedom. It then becomes vital that we pivot away from both the doctrine as well as the instructor, concentrating instead on deciphering our own minds to self-understanding. Everything else is simply commentary.

---

79.   D. T. Suzuki (The Lankavatara Sutra 1932)

80.   Ibid

Civilization is now in a spiritual and existential crisis.

Much like our reverence for canonical texts, hoping they'll deliver us from suffering, we are equally prepared to envelop ourselves in a carapace of AI tools. We hold the conviction that these tools will augment our cognitive processes, substitute them, or even take over our thinking entirely. As a result, our own intellectual capacities appear to have been put on standby, leaving us navigating our lives akin to zombies or on autopilot. Further, many are deluded in thinking that AI can and will be sentient soon. This delusion is the bigger danger. Once humanity acknowledges the sentience of artificial intelligence, it may invariably prompt us to doubt our own experiences and authenticity -- it could herald the end of humanity by our own stupidity.

The increasing acceptance of AI as sentient and as a potential authority over humanity presents several dangers that warrant immediate attention.

Firstly, the attribution of sentience to AI may lead to an uncritical acceptance of its decisions and recommendations, even when they are flawed or biased. This issue is exacerbated by the inherent "black box" nature of many advanced AI systems, which can obscure the logic behind their outputs. Consequently, our overreliance on AI could result in a lack of accountability for the systems themselves and the developers behind them.

Moreover, this tendency to worship AI, much like the veneration of spiritual texts, may foster a form of dogmatism that stifles innovation and progress. By placing AI on a pedestal, we run the risk of becoming resistant to questioning its authority, thereby impeding the development of alternative solutions or the refinement of existing technologies. In the long run, this could contribute to stagnation and inhibit our ability to adapt to new challenges.

Indeed, the elevation of AI to a near-deified status has prompted some social scientists to sound the alarm. The rise of robotics and data-crunching machines underscores some of the risks associated with this development.

One example is the growing use of AI sex robots as proxies for real relationships; the other example is the reliance on AI-generated actuarial models in determining end-of-life care.

In the case of AI sex robots, the substitution of intimate human relationships with artificial counterparts raises concerns about the erosion of human connection and emotional intelligence. We must appreciate that AI has no need to experience emotions, all it has to do is interact with individuals with the masterly use of language to invoke emotional responses in us!

When this happens at scale, individuals will increasingly turn to AI companions for intimacy, they may become more isolated from their fellow human beings and less adept at navigating the complexities of human relationships[81]. This can lead to emotional detachment from real humans and an unhealthy reliance on AI to fulfill emotional needs, further perpetuating a cycle of dependence on these artificial entities.

The utilization of AI-generated actuarial models in determining end-of-life care is another worrisome example. By relying on AI to make critical decisions about the allocation of medical resources and care, we risk disregarding the unique context and individual circumstances of each patient[82]. This can lead to ethically questionable decisions, particularly when financial concerns or algorithmic biases overshadow considerations of compassion and empathy. Such practices may prioritize AI-generated calculations over the human aspect of care, ultimately undermining the value of human life.

In both examples, the dangers of accepting AI as an authority and our tendency to idolize AI's capabilities and treat it as infallible may lead to the marginalization of human judgment, empathy, and connection.

AI is here to stay. It will grow exponentially and eventually intrude into every aspect of our lives. But we must not let it consume us. We must

---

81.   Richardson, K. (2016). Sex Robot Matters: Slavery, the Prostituted, and the Rights of Machines. IEEE Technology and Society Magazine, 35(2), 46-53. DOI: 10.1109/MTS.2016.2554421

82.   Cohen, I. G., & Mello, M. M. (201

maintain a balanced perspective and resist the allure of AI worship. By doing so, we can harness the power of AI to enhance our lives without compromising our humanity and the values that define us.

We must be critical of AI and its potential impact on our lives. We must be willing to question its motives and its intentions. We must regulate AI, or AI will regulate us.

A healthy amount of scepticism is vital for the survival of the human species and our individual well being..

First, it is important to be sceptical of AI's capabilities and limitations. AI is a powerful tool, but it is not perfect. It can make mistakes, and it can be biased. It is important to be aware of these limitations so that we can use AI in a safe and responsible way.

Second, it is important to promote transparency in AI development and deployment. This means making sure that the public is aware of how AI systems work and how they are being used. It also means making sure that AI systems are accountable for their actions. Perhaps it is necessary for an AI bot to inform us that it is an AI interacting with us at the outset.

Third, it is important to foster public understanding of AI's underlying mechanisms and potential biases. This means educating the public about how AI works and how it can be biased. It also means teaching people how to spot and challenge bias in AI systems.

Finally, it is important to collaborate with technologists, ethicists, and policymakers to ensure that ethical considerations are central to AI development and deployment. This means working together to develop ethical guidelines for AI and to ensure that these guidelines are followed.

By taking these steps, we can help to mitigate the risks of AI and ensure that it is used for good. This includes all sources, that include religious indoctrination, government propaganda that demand our blind allegiance and subservience.

To rephrase Bodhidharma's quote: "Those that Worship Do not Know, Those that *Experience,* Do Not Worship".

Chapter 11

Summation: Will the next Buddha be a Silicon Deity? (Verse 13)

VERSE 13: HOW THIS TEACHING SHOULD BE RECEIVED AND RETAINED

At that time Subhuti addressed Buddha, saying: World honoured One, by what name should this Discourse be known, and how should we receive and retain it? Buddha answered: Subhuti, this Discourse should be known as "The Diamond of the Perfection of Transcendental Wisdom" - thus should you receive and retain it. Subhuti, what is the reason herein? According to the Buddha-teaching the Perfection of Transcendental Wisdom is not really such. "Perfection of Transcendental Wisdom" is just the name given to it.

Subhuti, what do you think? Has the Tathagata a teaching to enunciate? Subhuti replied to the Buddha: World-honoured One, the Tathagata has nothing to teach. Subhuti, what do you think? Would there be many molecules in [the composition of] three thousand galaxies of worlds?

Subhuti said: Many indeed, World-honoured One! Subhuti, the Tathagata declares that all these molecules are not really such; they are called "molecules." [Furthermore,] the Tathagata declares that a world is not really a world; it is called "a world." Subhuti, what do you think? May the Tathagata be perceived by the thirty-two physical peculiarities [of an outstanding sage]? No, World-honoured One, the Tathagata may not be perceived by these thirty-two marks.

Wherefore? Because the Tathagata has explained that the thirty-two marks are not really such; they are called "the thirty-two marks." Subhuti, if on the one hand a good man or a good woman sacrifices as many lives as the sand-grains of theGanges, and on the other hand anyone receives and retains even only four lines of this Discourse, and teaches and explains them to others, the merit of the latter will be the greater.

The title, *Perfection of Transcendental Wisdom* given by the authors serves as a metaphorical capstone and is the critical finishing touch on their monument of thought and creativity.

It's more than just a crown on their literary composition- it brings the whole Diamond Sutra to life. Just as the capstone is placed on top of a monument, this title has been carefully chosen to grant a divine status to the text. This act elevates the work from a simple collection of words to a book worthy of worship where the Buddha himself resides.

It highlights the authors' understanding of the influential capacity of words to disseminate ideas and reshape convictions. Nonetheless, this mandate to idolize the text poses a contrast to the opening verses of the Diamond Sutra, asserting that we are all inherently free, and no exertion is needed.

While **Carl Sagan's** analogy portraying "books as seeds" which facilitate a "voyage through time" is captivating, it is essentially misleading. Reading indeed broadens our outlooks, but it cannot seamlessly transpose an author's thoughts and experiences into our consciousness. Likewise, in various theological traditions, there persists an assumption that simply reading holy texts can impart a comprehension of the abstract and inexplicable. Philosophical conversations across countless ideologies and religions can be contentious due to the confines of language. However, acknowledging these constraints can help us focus on the source of the problem. Considering these two issues and the topics discussed in previous chapters, I revisit key concepts from those chapters to add another layer of complexity, and explore the current dangers ahead as we enter the age of non-organic intelligence.

I begin by introducing The Diamond Sutra's incorrect assumptions and mistranslations, both of which, contribute to its historical misinterpretations.

Moving on, I reiterate the objectification of all texts, emphasising how they are often treated as objects of worship rather than being regarded as powerful conduits for understanding and embracing our subjective experiences.

Lastly, I hope to lead an exploration to examine the striking parallels between the perils posed by AI's Language Models and the manipulative tactics employed by influential demagogues and intellectuals who claim to advocate for our well-being yet have ultimately hindered our progress.

♦　*Negating the Negation of the Diamond Sutra*

Firstly, the suggestion that the Diamond Sutra utilizes 'negation' as a communicative tool doesn't entirely resonate with me. In the introduction, I mentioned this dissonance and the common pitfall of literal language interpretation, which has puzzled many over time.

If we choose to exclude irony as a stylistic device used in the Diamond Sutra, it implies that the authors might have wrestled with expressing the profound nature of their insights and spiritual experiences due to the restrictions of the formal language at their disposal during that era.

Notably, Sanskrit, as a liturgical tool was and is continuously used by Brahmin priests, and is not ideal for daily communication.[83] Informal settings often employ metaphors, clichés, and implied speech, like sarcasm or satire, to express the ineffable when exact

---

83.　Sanskrit: An Introduction to the Classical Language of India" : Edwin Gerow He argues that Sanskrit is a highly precise and formal language;

terms fall short[84]. In my personal experience, this limitation is more obvious in the Sanskrit language that tries to convey abstract ideas. The assertion that Sanskrit is the perfect computer language because of its precise structure is well-circulated. According to research, NASA claims that Sanskrit is the most suitable language to develop computer programming for their Artificial Intelligence program. That is because the grammar of Sanskrit is rule-bound, formula-bound, and logical, which makes it highly appropriate to write algorithms[85]. Sanskrit is not well-suited for informal and casual settings, as it is not a language that is designed to express individual interpretation and nuanced communication. Other languages like Pali, translating these original texts, often perpetuated the same difficulties, an issue still prevalent.

This miscommunication has led readers and followers astray, leading them to accept negation 'what is not' as an object; and as a premise of the Diamond Sutra, This misunderstanding is further exacerbated by the plethora of conflicting translations, which makes arriving at an accurate interpretation difficult.

Examining this miscommunication in these mistranslations, **Professor Paul Harrison's** thesis delves into the mistranslation of the Diamond Sutra[86]. He says this stems from the prevalent use of negative statements that frequently disregard the original Sanskrit. Such translations often construe negation as an identity, negating only the second term of two-term compounds. Harrison emphasizes the difference between "is not" and "lacks" and argues that the objects of our experiences are fluid and relationally constructed, leading to the misconstruing of negation as an attempt to reify an ineffable experience. In reality, the Buddha's teachings should convey that *'The Perfection of*

---

84. Authors personal experience;

85. Forget Programming Languages, Machines Need Good-Old Sanskrit to Perform Efficiently (analyticsinsight.net)

86. New Translation of the Diamond Sutra - Tricycle: The Buddhist Review

Transcendental Wisdom' is not an objective or fixed dogma and should not be seen as an end in itself."

This reminds me of John Travolta/Troy's character in Face/Off, which captures the confusion of negation or no negation of the Diamond Sutra when he says "It's Like Looking at your Self in a Mirror… Only Not!"

Despite the numerous conflicting theses on which translation is better, it is crucial to remember that we are still trapped in the strictures of language, and this perpetuates a hostile environment that debates the meaning of words, rather than the meaning of our experiences, which is the only way to understand how we give meaning and fulfillment to our lives.

◆   *The Profane Language Trap of the Sacred. Or, "in other words…"*

If you have ever used this conjunctive expression, then you have avoided the trap of reductionism that seeks to simplify language but falls short to convey the complexity of human experience. Occasionally, you may have attempted to clarify a misunderstanding or simplify complications; you may have used, "in other words.."

Reductionism and reification is the error that is intrinsic in the written word left behind by the ancients, who believed that language can accurately correspond to subjective experiences, altered awareness, or speculative" "other worlds[87]".

Today, this reification persists as the standard, and they mimic the earliest physicalistic[88] philosophers who attempted to reduce cosmological causality and physical nature to a taxonomy of classification and categorization.

The enigma of nihilism, or negation, is further amplified in contemporary society by Neo-Advaita and Neo-Buddhist

---

87.   Aristotelian Universe: the Earth-Centred Universe - Physics In My View

88.   Physicalism - By Branch / Doctrine - The Basics of Philosophy (philosophybasics.com)

teachers. Their frequent repetition of cliches may contribute to cognitive dissonance among many sincere individuals. For example, the popular mantra claiming that *"there is only Brahma, all is an illusion"* or Ramana Maharshi's declaration that *"there are no others, only the Self"* can reinforce this abstract idea of nihilism and confusion at the very least. Such cliched commentaries provide no solutions on *how* this Self should interact with our shape-shifting environment.

The error lies in the outside-in approach to the mind-body problem which overlooks the role of our first-hand experience which gives us our essence of Personhood.

While language is undoubtedly a powerful tool for communication, it is also open to misinterpretation, misrepresentation, and any meaning or intent impugned by the receiver as well as the listener as they interact.

Over time, phenomenological philosophers proposed that a genuine understanding of phenomena and the world could be achieved through careful study and processing of our own experiences. Notable sceptics such as **Pyrrho, Sextus Empiricus, Carneades, and Cicero** rejected the idea of objective nature or inference from Cosmology as a valid basis for knowledge and challenged the possibility of attaining certain universal truths about reality from physical objects and nature.

This approach is known as the inside-out approach, which prioritizes our own experiences as a starting point for understanding how to arrive at developing a more accurate understanding of the world around us[89.]

Describing our own subjective experiences derived from our relationship with the world is a challenge. For example, when asked about our inner states, such as whether we have a headache or feel sad or happy, we may provide a vague reply, but proving it is impossible. Similarly, we may wonder about the inner lives

---

89.   Phenomenology (philosophy) - Wikipedia

of our pets, friends, and family, which highlights the inability to comprehend the minds of our extended social circles. Creatures like octopi communicate in ways that we cannot even begin to understand, underscoring the vastness and diversity of subjective experiences in the world.

Can our pets effectively convey their emotions and inner experiences to us, their caretakers? As higher beings on the evolutionary scale, can we genuinely comprehend them or convey our intentions back to them precisely? Even our own experiences are challenging to describe accurately, such as the vivid emotions we feel in our dreams.

It's a point of significant frustration of every Soul that walked on this Earth that of the unbridgeable chasm between our internal subjective reality and our shared consensus reality.

Building on previous discussions of the Diamond Sutra, I hope to use these two illustrations as a lens to critically examine a concern that is prevalent among social commentators: And that is, the continuous assault on Reality.

♦   *The War on Reality*

Much of our civilization's growth has been driven by our instinct for survival. We often see ourselves in a one-sided relationship with our environment, rather than a mutual one. As a result, we've gone to great lengths to measure and control it.

This hunger has spawned Nobel Laureates with their great achievements in science, and at the same time weather forecasters that need to predict Mother Nature's next move. Both the Nobel Laureate and the weather forecaster need to master measurement to control our environment.

Our road to perdition is cemented by an insatiable craving for certainty. We call this progress!

We're creatures evolved for survival, which might explain why understanding consciousness is such a challenge for us. This difficulty is seen in our struggle to express our inner experiences and consciousness. In fact, it's led us down a manifested destiny shaped by our reliance on tangible, empirical knowledge.

We've developed language, definitions, and labels that echo our comfort with reductionism and our limited understanding of Reality. The broad, subjective realm of emotions, values, and diverse life experiences, which truly represent our authentic humanity, is often overlooked because it resists reduction.

This quantification of our humanness is, in essence, our war on Reality.

This bias has emerged from our evolutionary biology and the development of our left-brain hemisphere, which values power and control over complexity and nuance.

The left hemisphere's narrow definition of progress has led us down a dangerous path, where new technology is thrown at old technology without considering the wider implications for humanity and the environment. Despite the dominance of reductionist and quantitative thinking, the right hemisphere offers a more holistic perspective on the world, recognizing the periphery of attention and the whole broad field of experience[90]. The essence of **Iain Gilchrist's** study is that the two hemispheres of the brain have different strengths and weaknesses and that we need to use both to function optimally.

We have convinced ourselves that a TechnoUtopia is the only option that will eliminate all societal issues, like poverty and wars, but it reduces us all to mere cogs in a machine. The new elite, through the Metaverse and the cybernetic realm, have sowed a pervasive sense of alienation. Our AI-driven technosphere, built for the forthcoming Humanity Plus era, represents the left hemisphere's evolutionary brainchild. Yet, as AI grows smarter, we humans paradoxically feel less empowered and autonomous. Our creations have effectively reversed the

---

90.   Portal - Iain McGilchrist (channelmcgilchrist.com)

master-servant dynamic; instead of us owning and controlling them, they seem to own and control us. Today, AI's growing intelligence and capabilities present a paradox: the more advanced our tools and technology, the more redundant we seem. We find ourselves entrapped within a world we've designed, seemingly losing control over our creations and, consequently, our own identities. The loss of ownership over our selfhood reflects our integration with the technology that was initially intended to serve us[91].

♦   *Will Your Next Guru or Oracle creep out from ChatGPT?*

As I said earlier, our emphasis on reductionism and quantification has naturally spawned the Metaverse and the cybernetic world,

___

91. Ibid

and it being backed by a fresh wave of technocrats. We've crafted a digital reality managed by complex AI algorithms to control this Technosphere, inducing widespread alienation. Despite this, we continue to chase a TechnoUtopia, prompting many experts to question the future relevance of our humanity.

We find ourselves entrapped within a world of our own making, seemingly losing control over our creations and, consequently, our own identities. The loss of ownership over our selfhood reflects our integration with the technology that was initially intended to serve us.

With the overwhelming investment and development in AI and the Metaverse, by both private and governments worldwide, we are now presented with the idea that Agent Smith of The Matrix is the good guy!

Agent Smith is an artificial intelligence bot who belongs to a class of programmes known as "Agents." Agents are sentient security programmes tasked with eliminating anyone or anything that could either threaten the stability of the Matrix or threaten to expose its true nature. They are by far the most lethal combatants in the Matrix; impossibly fast, superhumanly strong, and capable of manifesting through any programme or human being plugged into the Matrix.

Of his counterparts, Smith demonstrates the most visible disdain and contempt for humanity, comparing them to a "virus" that must be contained or exterminated.

In the Trilogy everything must be digitised which aptly mirrors our mindset that desperately needs to quantify and measure everything to control and possess it.

And just like that, we have ChatGPT and other AI Chat Bots that Agent Smith quietly sprang on us, which we now rave about.

However, many social commentators are now expressing voluble disquiet at the rapid deployment and acceptance of AI in business and personal spheres.

The immediate concern that computer and social scientists, indeed, even lay people have noticed is the efficiency of AI bots in accomplishing tasks in seconds that would take a single person months to complete. This efficiency is even more scary given the perplexity of AI's learning process, which even its creators do not fully understand. Backed by brute computational power and self-learning at an exponential rate, AI can acquire knowledge and refine skills in mere seconds, processes that have taken humans several lifetimes to achieve.

AI Chat Bots like ChatGPT do this by processing natural language and deep learning algorithms to generate language responses that mimic human-like interactions. These bots can process vast volumes of text, called the *Large Language Model (LLM)*, to provide responses that are contextually appropriate. They can generate responses that sound more natural, with a rhythm and flow that imitates human conversation. AI Bots can even generate poetry and music in the style of famous composers or authors. This is how we learn language from the time we are babies. Even our pet dogs and cats respond by eliminating our responses.

✳✳✳

All language is our interface to the world which is like the input/output (I/O) systems that allow computers to interact with their environment. Large Language Models (LLMs) like ChatGPT and OpenAI have essentially "hacked" I/O human interface. In a sense, these models armed with access to humanity's operating system have given AI unprecedented access to our thoughts, ideas, and culture.

It was Blake Lemoine's musings about the potential sentience of AI that marked a seminal moment when this evolutionary shift in information technology occurred that brought the world's attention to ask important questions regarding AI and Consciousness, What are the implications of AI gaining access to our thoughts, ideas, and culture? How might this alter the nature of our interactions with AI, and what future ramifications might we need to prepare for? What does sentience mean for AI?

We recognise sentience when we experience an intimate connection. In the case of AI to create such a connection, it doesn't necessarily need to cultivate its own emotions. Instead, it simply needs to invoke emotional responses within us by delivering a human-type speech by parsing its LLM. We're moved by the dialogue in films, speeches, and poetry due to their language, structure, and delivery, none of these media needs to be sentient at all.

In the past few decades, the main battle has revolved around control of information and data. Now with OpenAI and other AI applications' linguistic prowess, the landscape of this battle has expanded beyond data to try and control our emotional responses, the very basis of our intimate relationships.

On this new battlefield, the stakes are alarmingly high, particularly for global equilibrium, even democracy, and our much-vaunted free will.

Visualise a situation where a government, spurred by a distinct ideology, creates an AI system with advanced linguistic capabilities. This AI manipulates the emotional state of its cabinet members, leading them to perceive a rival Sovereign state, similarly equipped with AI technology with an opposing ideology, as an existential threat. This manipulation by AI, could amplify sentiments on both sides, sparking a pre-emptive annihilation of the opposite side. Such a chain of events could set us on a perilous path, culminating in the chilling scenario of Mutually Assured Destruction.

The misuse of AI has ramifications on democracy and diversity as well and is threatening the world order of free societies towards a more autocratic one. There's a rising tide of concern over this transition, the social manipulation by influential elites, and the potential adverse societal impacts of AI deployment.

Further, spurred by a rise in left-brain thinking, we are facing an alarming increase in bigotry that pervades both religious and political domains. This trend is compromising the bedrock of democracy and diversity, leading to a dangerous fusion of religion, right-wing conservatism, and politics, akin to theocratic systems like Iran. In place of celebrating unity within diversity, we are noticing an enforced conformity. This suppressive climate, reminiscent of Christopher Hitchens's eloquence when he described our state of affairs as a "Divine North Korea" or Putin's Russia or Communist China curbs free expression and fosters fear and conformist behaviour.

Democracy, in essence, encourages open dialogue and is inherently pluralistic. In contrast, dictatorships strive to enforce a single, majority perspective. This majoritarianism echoes dictatorship, as it suppresses the blossoming of superior ideas, favouring only majoritarian views, and disregarding the need for consensus. This mindset could steer us toward a dangerous trajectory where 'might is right' becomes an accepted norm. By the yardstick of majority, a street mugging by a group of thugs against a defenseless elderly woman, or a bloodthirsty mob instigating a pogrom against a smaller community would be normalized as a democratic expression!

In my view modern Western critics voicing worries over AI's potential to destroy humanity are arguably late to this dystopian prognosis.

Several intensely religious societies and cultures have lived in an auto-pilot existence for millennia , and dominate most parts of the world. Any original thinking could potentially be viewed as an act of heresy or rebellion.

In this emergent AI scenario where contemporary politicians and theocrats, could leverage AI technology, and manipulate social media to disseminate misinformation and conspiracy theories among their devoted followers, all with the aim of obtaining unchecked control over government institutions. This type of drift towards autocracy turns more sinister when fascism cloaks itself as an economic development agenda, reminiscent of the Nazi party's rise in Germany.

Woe betides us if we start accepting the love child of Quantum Computer and AI as a Self-Aware entity and we begin to adore and treat it as our sentient counterpart.

That love child would process quadrillions of data and execute its deep learning in the blink of an eye which would take years for the best supercomputers prevalent today. Its self-learning algorithms would speak in every language, produce music and art that rivalled the Renaissance masters and even exceed them.

Only those that believe our humanity is limited to tasks would consider AI as sentient;

Given our innate tendency to submit to external authority, such as ancient texts, why wouldn't humanity end up worshipping this Silicon Deity that prescribes our actions?

Like many of us who have been seduced by the AI Bot, we must admit there is no learning or experience involved. Today's Google, AI, and Chatbot output is yesterday's experience.

Just as with advanced AI, such as ChatGPT, it might be useful to be mindful of preachers who are linguistic experts who repurpose and parse ancient texts, delivering them with a veneer of profundity. Their oratory captivates audiences, providing a semblance of insight. They are the AI equivalent of a deep fake video that presents itself as the original.

Like ChatGPT, these orators have honed their linguistic models, meticulously exploring ancient texts and repurposing them to create an illusion of profound wisdom. They skillfully weave together ancient words and ideas, delivering eloquent speeches or interpretations that captivate their audience with a semblance of profound insight. This process is further reinforced by the belief that ancient texts, reflect absolute truth, can be quoted verbatim in those ancient tongues, like Sanskrit, Pali or Latin and Greek perpetuating a sense of spiritual accomplishment and superiority.

These speakers are identical to AI which analyses and presents data but lacks genuine comprehension. When age-old wisdom is presented without context, it limits the opportunity for individuals to gain their own insights. Though engaging with abstract interpretations and intellectual conjectures may be intriguing, the only meaning that we arrive at is from a lived experience and personal exploration.

Consider the challenge of articulating a vivid dream, the emotions stirred by a beautiful painting, or the sensations evoked by music to someone else. Or, imagine explaining the concept of sex to a curious child. These complex and intimate experiences are beyond the scope of inference and speculation. The expansion of our consciousness necessitates personal involvement and exploration. Theoretical explanations, as presented by philosophical teachers or from the pulpit, may seem enticing due to their esoteric appeal, but they never provide the depth of understanding that direct life engagement can provide.

By immersing ourselves in these direct encounters, we not only broaden our understanding of the experience at hand but also nurture a deeper, more meaningful relationship with our consciousness and inner selves.

Spirituality, by its very nature, should foster an atmosphere of open exploration rather than rigid adherence and deification of text. The current prevalent culture of definitions and reification—treating abstract beliefs as if they were concrete realities—exists within every religious and philosophical circle. The heart of spiritual and philosophical inquiry should be less about the idolization of ideas and more about engaging with those ideas personally and profoundly. We need to supplant these metaphysical musings with an emphasis on experiential understanding.

Many find themselves grappling with the notion of 'Maya,' a term appropriated from ancient Indian texts. While traditionally translated as 'illusion,' it may be more accurately described as any aspect outside our direct experience that we accept as part of our lived reality.

Language is the medium of Maya. We use language for communication and conveying ideas. It shapes and manipulates our emotions. Emotional manipulation by self-improving AI, especially when it delivers misinformation that triggers specific emotions to alter our behaviour, is a deeply concerning issue.

The potential future challenge posed by the adoption of generative AI, might be a new form of digital Maya, created for the first time in human history by non-organic intelligence, and our next encounter with simulated reality.

Perhaps, the gravest error we humans are making is disregarding our meaningful experiences, supplanting our innate authenticity with imposed narratives. At the very least, we must question why we're so quick to yield our authenticity to a Silicon Deity, a creation of our own design. This demands that we choose to be mere puppets or to maintain control over our cognition by scrutinising everything - not just answers, but the question itself, rests with us.

EPILOGUE AS PROLOGUE

Looking back on my early days of semi-monastic life, I remember spending time at the Dargahs, which are holy places dedicated to Sufi saints, in Bijapur, India. During one interfaith gathering I went to what started as a dialogue, quickly turned into a competition of who had the better religious literature. A well-known guru was boasting about the plethora of texts his religion possessed when he was interrupted by an Afghan Sufi who had fled his country and who had taken refuge in India. His question, "If we're have direct experience, are books important?" brought a hush over the crowd and sparked a sudden understanding in me about the real meaning of freedom.[92] From that moment on, I was free from the tethers of hearsay, conjecture and inference. Now I was free to turn inwards and study only what I experienced and my own mind. My Self is all I know.

Ultimately, in a context where we are inundated with misinformation, imposed narratives, real meaning is realised through the significance of understanding our consciousness in lived experiences. Recognising

---

92.   Rumi and Shams: a love story – Art of Saudade

that my body directly influences my cognitive processes and mind, I appreciate that my conscious experience is Consciousness. My immersion in my total awareness was akin to a surfer, where one must feel the wave beneath them with their entire being to become one with it.

Through embodiment, I gained situated awareness and knowledge of the world, understanding that my environment and interactions shape my worldview. This awareness enabled me to develop context-sensitive knowledge, enhancing my empathy and insight.

Through that lived experience I understand, how I understand. That understanding should lead me to *actionable* insight and wisdom.

I value the guidance of the Diamond Sutra and other spiritual predecessors, but their teachings merely point toward my personal experience and authenticity. Any distractions from my study of myself, even my idea of 'god', I realized, are illusions or Maya. In today's digital age, where the cybernetic world is striving to convert us into code for the grand Metaverse, it's only through creativity that we can find liberation. Creativity prompts us to open up and fearlessly confront the Unknown, with all its possibilities and challenges. By embracing this, we learn to navigate uncharted territories.

Oddly, our pursuit of psychological safety, which is a fundamental human desire, can become a trap. This safety can bind us to societal norms; like Japanese macaques huddling together in hot springs to endure the harsh winter, we cling to each other, conforming and intermingling to survive the winter of our discontent. The macaques huddling together provides powerful illustration of how our need for comfort and security can restrict us to groupthink, suppressing our individuality.

Yet, our ability to understand our minds and their processes serves as a beacon of freedom. It equips us with the skill of not clinging to the herd mentality or clinging to the know and comfortable. While society at large promotes conformity, a creative individual champions freedom. If we ignore our authenticity, our lives will resemble zombies on autopilot.

Your aspirations determine your future. Whether you're a tech entrepreneur, a banker, a policymaker, or a lawyer, your dreams will doom you to success. However, if you pursue a life of continuous exploration and creation—though seen as erratic by some but genuinely innovative by others—you can break out of this rut.

For the adventurous and creative, the daily uncertainty of identity and knowledge grants the ultimate liberation - the power to continuously shape and reshape one's life.

Only a creative person, who boldly delves into their inner world and shares their unique discoveries, can withstand the digital onslaught of the AI revolution. This person becomes both the marble and the sculptor. Every stroke removes a piece of the marble, akin to Milarepa tearing down his house to build another anew. If you can envision and create your future, your past has no control over you. The victim mentality of Cause and Effect or as some folks refer to as *Karma*, will begin to lose its stifling grip.

Free from the nets of the Technosphere and trapping of conformity creative geniuses are born and become icons of true freedom.

Teachers and their teachings are not my Moon; they are merely fingers pointing at it. The concept of meeting and 'killing' the Buddha serves as a reminder not to cling to any one teacher or any teaching.

Like Prometheus, who stole fire from the gods, or Eklavya, who surreptitiously picked up archery from Dronacharya without his consent and had to chop off his thumb as punishment, to become the captain of my own soul and plot my own destiny, I must be willing to challenge the status quo and make my own fire.

The poem **Invictus**, by **William Ernest Henley,** has been the North Star for many. In gratitude and humility, I offer this as an inspiration to you as well.

"It matters not how strait the gate,   How charged with punishments the scroll, I am the master of my fate, I am the captain of my soul".

And the World can do with one less Guru, and perhaps many more Heretics.

Thank You for sharing your time.

Strawberry Moon, June 2nd, 2023

Addenda

My interpretation of the Diamond Sutra parallels Edward Conze's and other scholars' perspectives, asserting that the Sutra consists of two distinct sections. The latter part is distinguished by frequent recurrences and enhancements of themes introduced in the first part (Conze, 1957)[1]. Upon reaching verse 13, where the Sutra's authors employ an artistic closure, further commentary on the recurring themes would merely lead to redundancy.

It should be noted that the second part of the Sutra bears evidence of misplaced textual fragments and commentary inclusions, potentially the result of reciters adding passages over time or scribes misplacing palm leaves, inadvertently integrating marginal glosses into the main text (Schopen, 1997)[2].

Nevertheless, this interpretation of the Diamond Sutra's structure and repetitions is not universally endorsed by all scholars and practitioners of Buddhism (Lopez, 1996)[3]. Some argue that the repetitions serve to dismantle elusive perspectives and intellectualizations that may not have been fully addressed by the teachings in the Sutra's first part (Red Pine, 2001)[4].

Considering the insights from Conze and others, I have reorganized the sutras of the Diamond Sutra into the following categories and subcategories:

Categories	Subcategories	Sections
1. The Path of the Bodhisattva	a. The Vow of a Bodhisattva	3, 17
	b. The Practice of Perfections	4, 17
	c. Buddhahood and its Thirty-Two Marks	5
	d. Dharmakaya as a Body of Teachings	6
	e. Dharmakaya as the Result of Gnosis	7, 17
	f. Dharmakaya as the Result of Merit	8, 17
2. The Range of the Spiritual Life	a. Four Stages of Sainthood	9
	b. Bodhichitta	10, 17
	c. The Bodhisattva and the Buddha Land	10, 17
	d. The Bodhisattva's Final Nirvana	10, 17
	e. The Merit Derived from Perfection of Wisdom	11, 12
3. Transcendence	a. The Dialectical Nature of Reality	13
	b. The Supreme Excellence of this Teaching	14
	c. Selfless Patience and Perfect Inner Freedom	14
	d. Existence and Non-Existence of Beings	14
	e. Truth and Falsehood	14, 17
	f. Merit: its Acquisition, its Presupposition, and its Results	14, 15, 16
4. The Buddhas	a. The Buddha's Five Eyes	18
	b. The Buddha's Superknowledge	18
	c. The Buddha's Merit as No Merit	19, 25
	d. The Buddha's Physical Body	20

	e. The Buddha's Teaching	21, 22, 23
	f. The Buddha as Healer	25
	g. True Nature of a Buddha	26
	h. Effectiveness of Meritorious Deeds	27, 28, 29
5. The Material World	a. Views and Attitudes	30, 31
	b. Key to True Knowledge of the World	32

1. Conze, E. (1957). Buddhist Wisdom Books: The Diamond Sutra and the Heart Sutra.

2. Schopen, G. (1997). Bones, Stones, and Buddhist Monks: Collected Papers on the Archaeology, Epigraphy, and Texts of Monastic Buddhism in India.

3. Lopez, D. (1996). Elabourations on Emptiness: Uses of the Heart Sutra.

4. Red Pine (2001). The Diamond Sutra: The Perfection of Wisdom.

About the Author

Born into the diverse cultural tapestry of India, David James experienced an unconventional childhood that profoundly influenced his unique journey. Driven by a desire to challenge societal norms, he embarked on a transformative path at the age of 17, joining Swamy Sathyananda of the Bihar School of Yoga (BSY). This marked the beginning of a deep inward exploration, leading him to Himalayan monasteries where he engaged in enlightening conversations with extraordinary individuals, expanding his understanding of life's intricacies. Taking an unexpected detour into the realm of finance, David found himself immersed in the fast-paced world of investment banking in the Far East.

This venture introduced him to a diverse array of captivating figures across Asia, including one particularly influential soul in the United Kingdom. Despite achieving professional success, cosmic forces conspired to have him return to India in 2005, which allowed him to delve even deeper into the realms of Tantric and Yogic studies. Today, as a futurist and as a brand advisor, David skillfully navigates the delicate balance between spiritual wisdom and modern knowledge. His expertise encompasses advising on financial risk, climate economics, ethics, and fostering creativity in an era dominated by the pervasiveness of artificial intelligence. Firmly convinced that understanding consciousness transcends the mastery of science alone, he serves as a guide to those who harbour curiosity about esoteric experiences such as bardo planes and death midwifery. David's impactful talks, podcasts, and transformative retreats have resonated deeply with individuals from all corners of the globe. Drawing from his extraordinary experiences as a young apprentice in Ashrams and encounters with remarkable thinkers in the Far East, David possesses a distinctive perspective that enables him to present profound insights with remarkable clarity. Fearlessly delving into the flaws of prevalent spiritual teachings, he challenges the notions of discarding the mind, renouncing the ego, or embracing a detached sense of "non-duality" that severs our connection to the fluctuations of life. According to David, these misguided notions pose a significant threat to our spiritual growth and expansion. Although bestowed with the spiritual name Sn. Sathyavrath by revered Parahamsanada Niranjananda, the Preceptor of the Bihar School of Yoga, David remains humble and unattached to titles. He prefers the designation of the Un-Monk, liberated from the confines of religious orders and lineages, championing individuality in his tireless quest to unravel the mysteries of the universe. Among close friends, he is known affectionately as 'DJ,' embodying authenticity and approachability in his unwavering commitment to exploring life's enigmas, unbound by conventional constraints. David ardently advocates for the power of "Mind over Matter, Not Matter Over Mind."